Surprised by Mary

Surprised by Mary

*How the Christ Who Was Born through
Mary Can Be Born Again through You*

JAMES A. HARNISH

Foreword by Donna Claycomb Sokol

CASCADE *Books* • Eugene, Oregon

SURPRISED BY MARY
How the Christ Who Was Born through Mary Can Be Born Again through You

Copyright © 2024 James A. Harnish. All rights reserved. Except for brief quotations in critical publications or reviews, no part of this book may be reproduced in any manner without prior written permission from the publisher. Write: Permissions, Wipf and Stock Publishers, 199 W. 8th Ave., Suite 3, Eugene, OR 97401.

Cascade Books
An Imprint of Wipf and Stock Publishers
199 W. 8th Ave., Suite 3
Eugene, OR 97401

www.wipfandstock.com

PAPERBACK ISBN: 978-1-6667-7422-1
HARDCOVER ISBN: 978-1-6667-7423-8
EBOOK ISBN: 978-1-6667-7424-5

Cataloguing-in-Publication data:

Names: Harnish, James A. | Claycomb Sokol, Donna, foreword.

Title: Surprised by Mary : how the Christ who was born through Mary can be born again through you / James A. Harnish ; foreword by Donna Claycomb Sokol

Description: Eugene, OR : Cascade Books, 2024 | Includes bibliographical references.

Identifiers: ISBN 978-1-6667-7422-1 (paperback) | ISBN 978-1-6667-7423-8 (hardcover) | ISBN 978-1-6667-7424-5 (ebook)

Subjects: LCSH: Mary, Blessed Virgin, Saint—Theology. | Protestant churches—Doctrines.

Classification: BT613 .H37 2024 (paperback) | BT613 .H37 (ebook)

05/17/24

With gratitude for Randalyn C. Harnish and Freddie L. Hayes—
Mother by birth and Mother by marriage.

Oh yes, Lord, I am definitely your servant!
    I am your servant and the son of your female servant . . .
So I'll offer a sacrifice of thanksgiving to you,
    and I'll call on the Lord's name.
I'll keep the promises I made to the Lord
    in the presence of all God's people. (Ps 116:16–18)

Attending to Mary gives one a heightened awareness of the suffering of the world. There is something about Mary's story that gives one eyes to see with fresh anguish the world we are living in.

–Jerusha Matsen Neal[1]

My dear children, I feel the pangs of childbirth all over again till Christ be formed within you.

—Gal 4:19, Phillips

---

1 Personal correspondence.

Contents

	Permissions	ix
	Foreword by Donna Claycomb Sokol	xi
	Introduction	xiii
1	Bearing the Impossible Promise	1
2	Birthing the New Creation	22
3	Breaking the Heart	40
4	Beginning at the End	60
5	Bending the Time	78
6	Becoming the Hope	94
	Epilogue	113
	Bibliography	123

Permissions

Scripture quotations not otherwise marked are from the Common English Bible. Copyright 2011 Common English Bible. Used by permission.

Scripture quotations marked NRSV are from the New Revised Standard Version Bible, copyright 1989 National Council of Churches of Christ in the United States of America. Used by permission. All rights reserved.

Scripture quotations marked MSG are taken from THE MESSAGE. Copyright by Eugene Peterson, 1993, 1994, 1995, 1996, 2000, 2001, 2002. Used by permission of NavPress Publishing Group.

Scripture quotations marked KJV are taken from the King James Version of the Bible.

Scripture quotations marked (GNT) are from the Good News Translation in Today's English Version—Second Edition Copyright © 1992 by American Bible Society. Used by Permission.

Scripture quotations marked MOFF are taken from James Moffatt's translation *The New Testament* (New York: Association, 1922).

Scripture quotations marked TEV are from Today's English Version, copyright 1976 American Bible Society. Used by permission. All rights reserved.

Scripture quotations marked Phillips are from J.B. Phillips's translation *The New Testament in Modern English* (London: Geoffrey Bles, 1960).

Scripture passages marked AP are the author's paraphrase.

Foreword

Words about Mary are often penned by feminist theologians, Roman Catholic priests, or women who can describe firsthand the sensation of life moving within their womb. While Jim Harnish is none of these things, his ministry as a Protestant pastor is one that has cultivated surprising new life within young adults who relinquished their successful careers to say "yes" to a call to ordained ministry, countless women who have been given the opportunity to faithfully birth new ministries that have touched a myriad of lives, and individuals who can testify to how Jim has helped them be a God-bearer, wherever they are.

I first met Jim on Sunday, September 16, 2001—five days after the horrific events of September 11. The sanctuary at Hyde Park United Methodist Church was overflowing with people who were eager to hear a word from the Lord that might bring comfort, healing, and peace. While I do not recall the passage of Scripture read that day, I do remember hearing a pastor who longed for his congregation to know that God was with them and would not let them go.

I was at Hyde Park in my role as director of admissions for Duke Divinity School. Hyde Park had been selected as one of the seminary's "Teaching Congregations," a place we would send our most gifted students for their summer field education placement. While there are many remarkable disciples at Hyde Park, the reason we wanted to send students to Tampa was to afford them the

Foreword

privilege of learning from Jim. Jim had a proven track record for faithfully starting a congregation in Orlando that continues to flourish today before leading the turnaround at Hyde Park, one he has written about in *You Only Have to Die*. The administration of the Divinity School knew Jim would provide an example of exceptional pastoral leadership through which students could be shaped into the kind of leader that could guide congregations into deep levels of faithfulness.

Twenty-two years later, I am grateful to call Jim a mentor and a friend. He has consistently named my God-given gifts, granting me the courage to believe I could lead a declining congregation into new life. Jim has regularly reminded me of how God was using me to birth Jesus' transformational love in the heart of the city. He has quickly cheered me on when he saw how Jesus was renewing a congregation's hope for their future. Countless times, Jim is the reason I was able to see how the Almighty is still doing great things in and through those who allow themselves to be used in seemingly surprising ways.

Jim now offers readers the gift of a journey with Mary that is filled with surprise, wonder, love, and justice. It is a journey from the heart of a pastor who knows how God continues to use ordinary women to do extraordinary things. It is a journey that leaves me saying, "Here am I, the servant of the Lord; let it be with me according to your word!"

Donna Claycomb Sokol
Pastor, Mount Vernon Place United Methodist Church
Washington, DC

Introduction

WHAT'S SO SURPRISING ABOUT MARY?

When was the last time you were surprised?

Sunday, December 7, 1941. Japanese fighter pilots took the nation by surprise when they attacked Pearl Harbor. When Bret Stephens looked back on the eightieth anniversary of that event, *The New York Times* columnist warned, "We are losing the capacity for surprise."[1]

New Testament scholar C. Kavin Rowe offered a similar warning to people who identify themselves as followers of Christ. He observed the way we "cut off the chance for surprise and renewal in our time with an assumption that we already know what the biblical God is or should be doing in the world."[2] He concluded, "If Christianity is anything at all like what the early sources claim it is, then woe to us if we forget its power, make it boring, and lose its surprise. Human life is just too hard to have a boring Christianity."[3]

I didn't think Mary could surprise me. I heard about her in sermons, songs, and prayers my entire life, particularly around Christmas and on Good Friday. She was like a church member I thought I knew well. But when we were preparing for this church member's memorial service, I was surprised to discover things about his life I had never known before. In the same way, as I listened more intently to the gospel stories about Mary, I discovered

---

1. Stephens, "Pearl Harbor," para. 1.
2. Rowe, *Christianity's Surprise*, 2.
3. Rowe, *Christianity's Surprise*, ix.

Introduction

new ways in which her story can become a transformational metaphor through which the Son of God, who was born into the world through her, can be born again through us.

You may be a person for whom I wrote this book if you are:

- a long-time Christian who is open to new discoveries about something you thought you already knew;
- a curious young adult who questions whether the Christian faith makes any actual difference in our world today;
- a faithful woman who may be surprised to learn that your experience as a woman can be a way for others to experience the presence of Christ;
- a Roman Catholic, former Catholic, or never Catholic who wonders why a male, Protestant preacher would dare to write about Mary;
- a member of a small group of people who likes to ask hard questions and dig deeper into the stories the Gospels tell; or
- a follower of Christ who has not lost the capacity for surprise!

If any of those descriptions fit you, you are among the people whose faces I imagined on the other side of my computer screen as I wrote this book.

An Audacious Affirmation

I sometimes call myself a "congenital Christian." I identify with Timothy, Paul's protégé in the New Testament, who received the faith from his mother and grandmother (2 Tim 1:5). The Christian faith has been as much a part of my life as the twin brother who surprised the world by arriving four minutes after I did. I can't remember a time before I believed what my parents believed and tried to live the way they and the church taught me to live. I've questioned it, pushed against it, probed it, stretched it, and followed it to places my forbears never expected, but it has always been a part of who I am.

INTRODUCTION

Despite living with this faith for more than three-quarters of a century, I continue to be surprised by the astonishing claim that the same Christ who was born into the world through Mary can be born again into the world through ordinary folks like any of the readers of this book. I'm intrigued by Paul's surprisingly visceral words, "My dear children, I feel the pangs of childbirth all over again till Christ be formed within you" (Gal 4:19, Phillips).

That's audacious stuff! Brazen! Bold! Not restricted to prior assumptions or ideas. Extravagantly original, daringly courageous, and, sometimes, downright frightening! The New Testament and the historic creeds of the church make the staggering assertion that the infinite, perfectly loving God was born into the world through the finite and very human body of a young woman named Mary. The Word beyond words—the life-giving Word who spoke creation into existence—became flesh through Mary's body and lived and died among us, so all of us can become the persons through whom the living Christ becomes flesh again.

If this affirmation has become so familiar that we've lost our capacity for surprise, it's become far too familiar. Discovering it anew is like folks on *Antiques Roadshow* who suddenly learn that the old book, painting, or piece of furniture that has been unnoticed in their home for years is valued at some astronomical amount.

There's nothing boring about the biblical story. The Old Testament is the surprising saga of the almighty God who engages in human history in unexpected, intrusive, and very physical ways. God works through the earthy, flesh-and-blood bodies of ordinary, imperfect people who become the extraordinary agents of God's saving, transforming, life-giving purpose at specific times and in finite places. The New Testament recounts the even more astonishing story of the God who "spoke through the prophets to our ancestors in many times and many ways . . . spoke to us through a Son" (Heb 1:1–2).

Luke's Gospel begins with two very ordinary women who, along with their gob-smacked husbands, are surprised by the unexpected promise that the infinite God would create new life

Introduction

through their very finite, human bodies. Matthew opens with the flabbergasting announcement that the child in Mary's womb was "conceived by the Holy Spirit" and would be called *Emmanuel*, which means "God with us" (Matt 1:20–23). Christian faith affirms that, in ways that confound easy explanation, the baby in Mary's womb was as much of God as could be squeezed into human flesh—dust to dust, birth to earth, womb to tomb. In Charles Wesley's powerful words, Jesus of Nazareth was "God contracted to a span, / Incomprehensibly made man."[4]

"But wait!" the TV hucksters shout in their infomercials. "There's more!"

The folks in Galatia must have been surprised (and perhaps offended) when Paul compared himself to a woman in labor praying for Christ to be formed in them like a fetus being formed in a woman's womb. Facing up to the fragility of their very human, dust-to-dust bodies, he told the Corinthians, "We always carry Jesus' death in our bodies so that Jesus' life can also be seen in our bodies" (2 Cor 4:10). He had the audacity to tell the Colossians that "the mystery" of God's purpose for the whole creation is realized in the promise, "Christ in you, the hope of glory" (Col 1:26–27, NRSV). The real Christ, really born into this real world through real bodies like yours and mine.

I was wrestling with this big idea when I heard Leonard I. Sweet make the same shocking assertion.

> The miracle of your calling is no less than the miracle of the birth of Jesus Christ through the virgin Mary.... Your calling is an impregnation of your life with the spirit of God and the Word of God becoming flesh in you. You have been called like Mary to give birth to the Christ child in your life. You are like Mary to bring Christ to this earth, to bring him alive in your life so that you can bring him to life in others.[5]

He echoed the words of Meister Eckhart, the thirteenth-century philosopher, theologian, and mystic: "We are all meant to

---

4. Wesley, "They Shall Call His Name," lines 5–6.
5. Sweet, "Amen."

Introduction

be mothers of God." He asked the intriguing question, "What good is it to me for the Creator to give birth to his Son if I do not also give birth to him in my time and my culture?"[6]

But *how* does that happen? Not literally "how" in terms of the unrepeatable, gynecological event through which a young woman in Nazareth became pregnant, but how do our bodies become the bodies through which Christ is born by the power of the Holy Spirit in our world today? How does the Word that became flesh in Jesus become a living, breathing, bleeding, laughing, loving, world-transforming Word through our flesh? What would it look like if people who affirm the Christian faith became the real presence of Jesus in our politically polarized, spiritually confused, and biblically illiterate world today?

This study is grounded in the conviction that Christ becomes flesh in us not in a miraculous moment of spiritual conception, but as we live into the stories recorded in the gospels. It grows out of the long narrative of God's relationship with the covenant people in the Hebrew Scriptures, as we apply the words of the Gospel to our experience by seeing the witness of faithful people who came this way before us. I invite you to join me in exploring some intriguing questions.

- What difference does it make to experience Jesus' story through Mary's story? How does Mary show us the way without becoming the central character in the story? The gospel is not about Mary, but about her Son.

- How can Mary's story become a transformative metaphor for the way we become the answer to Paul's impregnating prayer, "I'm going through labor pains again until Christ is formed in you" (Gal 4:19)?

- What if the Christian life is not only about how *we* can be "born again" but about how *Jesus* can be born again through us by the power of the Holy Spirit?

---

6. Eckhart, "Be Mothers of God," para. 1.

Introduction

A Man Walking Carefully

First, a disclaimer. It's a risky business for a man who has never experienced the mystery of conception, the weight of pregnancy, the labor of childbirth, or the lifelong joy and pain of motherhood, to write about Mary. I enter her story carefully, humbly, and treading lightly because of the inherent risk of falling into simplistic tropes or the culturally inherited assumption that everything that really matters flows in and through white, straight, male experience. We've had a couple millennia of that in the church!

On the Roman Catholic and Orthodox branches of the Christian family tree, veneration of Mary as the "Queen of Heaven" and "Blessed Mother" lifted her so far above our ordinary human experience that the same male priests who prayed *to* her have never allowed women *like* her to serve as priests who lead others in those same prayers. On the Protestant branch, we often see what Jason Byassee described to me as "the sort of anti-Catholicism that gets nervous to even let Mary back into the building for fear she'll take over."[7] Fundamentalists who claim the inerrant inspiration of Scripture often ignore the role of women in the same Scripture. Some refuse to ordain women to proclaim the story. A pastoral colleague who read an early draft of this material pointed out, "My anti-Roman Catholic New England Puritan ancestors have scared us away from considering Mary for about 400 years." She added, "Our puritan fears and prejudices may have kept us from a fuller experience of the gospel."

I'm neither a Roman Catholic nor a fundamentalist. I've served for half a century as a pastor in The United Methodist Church. My denomination began ordaining women nearly a century ago. We still have a long way to go in fully affirming women, persons of color, and members of the LGBTQ community in ministry, but we keep stumbling in the right direction.

In approaching Mary's story, I identify with the journalist Frye Gaillard. He was a 22-year-old reporter in Nashville when he asked the celebrated Native American author Vine Deloria Jr. if it

---

7. Personal correspondence.

Introduction

was presumptuous for a white reporter to cover the "Indian beat." Deloria responded "with extraordinary kindness" when he told him, "No, it's not presumptuous, as long as you listen."[8]

I've been listening to and learning from ruthlessly honest, spiritually thoughtful, personally courageous women throughout my life. Even as Mary was "overshadowed" by the Spirit, I've been overshadowed by Spirit-empowered women of faith who encouraged me in the past and energize my thinking in the present. For over fifty years I've been blessed by and accountable to my wife, Martha; our daughters, Carrie Lynn Ferenac and Deborah Jeanne LaRoche; and three of our five grandchildren who are all too rapidly becoming young women.

Jerusha Matsen Neal, professor of homiletics at Duke Divinity School, awakened me to the way Luke's account of Mary's "Spirit-empowered pregnancy" can become a living metaphor for "how our bodies relate to the Spirit's work and Christ's embodied presence."[9] She is among the women scholars and writers who have influenced this book. I will accomplish an ulterior purpose if I encourage you to discover the works of Ellen F. Davis, Rachel Held Evans, Kate Bowler, Diana Butler Bass, Amy Jill Lavine, and Lauren Winner. I'm grateful for the women who read and improved numerous drafts of this book including Andrea Batchelor, Deborah Galtere, Deborah (Harnish) LaRoche, Sandra Roughton, Deborah McLeod, Christine Parton Burkett, and Judith Harnish. Some of the men who helped sharpen my thinking include Magrey deVega, Irv Brendlinger, Nathan Kirkpatrick, John Harnish, Kavin Rowe, and my long-time friend, most honest critic, and faithful encourager, Dan G. Johnson.

Mary as Metaphor

A metaphor is a figure of speech that invites us to see an unfamiliar reality through a familiar one while never denying that they are

---

8. Gaillard, *Hard Rain*, 620.
9. Neal, *Overshadowed Preacher*, 21.

Introduction

not the same. Through metaphor, something we cannot literally experience becomes a reality as we participate in it. Metaphors work as we visualize them, smell them, taste them, feel the texture of them, and step into them. They are not self-proving like an experiment in a chemistry lab. They are self-authenticating when we connect who we are and what we experience with a reality that is other than our own.

Lauren Winner explored the way the Bible in general and Jesus in particular used metaphors to invite people to "look around their ordinary Tuesdays to see what they could see about holiness and life with God." She called metaphor "the Bible's way of making us aware of God and of the world in which we meet God."[10] Jesus used mothering as a metaphor in his parables. He portrayed himself as a mother hen gathering her chicks under her wings (Matt 23:37). The night before he died, he compared the grief his followers would feel at the cross to the pain of a woman in labor (John 16:20–22). Paul compared the suffering creation to a woman groaning in labor (Rom 8:18–25). The Old Testament prophet Isaiah heard the Lord cry as a woman in childbirth (Isa 42:14).

Jerusha Matsen Neal named the importance of seeing Mary as a metaphor rather than as a model. Mary's pregnancy is uniquely her own. None of us, regardless of gender or fertility, can literally know how Mary's baby was "conceived by the Holy Spirit." None of us can give birth to the Son of God the way Jesus burst from Mary's womb. With the horrifying exception of the mothers of lynching victims in both the past and the present, we have not seen our sons or daughters nailed to a cross. We cannot experience our child risen from the tomb. But this does not exclude us from finding ourselves in the stories the gospel writers include about her. By living into Mary's story, we can see our own story in a new and often surprising way. Her story becomes the door through which we step into a deeper relationship with Christ.

So, what do I bring to Mary's story? More importantly, what has Mary's story brought to me?

---

10. Winner, *Wearing God*, 16.

Introduction
==

The Power of a Secondhand Story

I was a blissful participant in the conception of two daughters and did my best to be a helpful partner during pregnancy. In those long-gone days when fathers were not permitted inside the delivery room, I missed out on their birth, except to be close enough to the delivery room door to hear our first daughter's first cry. I confess the obvious fact that my knowledge of pregnancy and childbirth is completely secondhand.

But secondhand is, after all, the only way we know Mary's story. She never wrote an autobiography, although any publisher or movie producer would give anything to get their hands on one! None of the gospel writers were present when the story they reported happened. They tell Mary's story as secondhand witnesses to the shocking way God took up residence among us from the moment the angel Gabriel intruded into Mary's life in Nazareth until the day of Pentecost when the Holy Spirit blew like the wind into the lives of Jesus' followers in the Upper Room. There's a lot more to Mary's story than the part we read at Christmas!

The gospels invite us to experience Mary as:

- a typical Jewish girl who is engaged to be married;
- a feisty young woman who questions God's word through Gabriel;
- a new mother who is equally surprised by the adoration of shepherds and the warning she receives from Simeon;
- a frustrated parent who worries about her missing teenage son;
- an anxious mother who, along with Jesus' siblings, intends to take Jesus home because he appears to be out of his mind;
- a grieving mother who watches her son die; and
- a faithful disciple who waits with Jesus' followers for the coming of the Spirit he promised.

Mary's story really matters. It's a deeply human story full of suffering and joy, darkness and danger, despair and hope. In the

Introduction

end, it's not so much a story we hold as a story that holds us. By watching how the Holy Spirit "overshadowed" Mary's life from Nazareth to the Upper Room, we can discover the same Spirit enabling us to become part of the great story of God's saving purpose for our lives and for the whole creation.

As we make this journey, I encourage you to be prepared for the way the Spirit of God may surprise you. In the end, this book is not as much about Mary as it is about Jesus. Pope John XXIII said, "The Madonna is not happy when she is placed before her son."[11] Finally, this is a book about the way the Holy Spirit, who enabled Christ to be born through Mary's body, can be at work to birth the presence of Christ through our bodies as well. With that hope, I invite you to join me in Phillips Brooks's Spirit-impregnating prayer:

> O Holy Child of Bethlehem,
> descend to us we pray;
> cast out our sin, and enter in,
> *be born in us today.*[12]

---

11. Van Biema, "Mary, So Contrary," 67.
12. Young, *United Methodist Hymnal*, 230, italics added.

1

Bearing the Impossible Promise

"You will conceive in your womb and bear a son." (Luke 1:31)

Have you ever received an invitation to be part of something that seemed impossible? When were you surprised because something you thought could never happen happened?

Conceiving a child was inconceivable to Mary. She knew that what needed to happen for pregnancy had not happened. But she was not the first woman in the biblical story to be surprised by an impossible, impregnating promise. Luke introduces Mary's story with the story of Elizabeth, another woman who never expected to be expecting a baby, along with Zechariah, her equally shell-shocked husband.

"They had no children, because Elizabeth was barren."
(Luke 1:7, NRSV)

If someone asked me to name the ugliest words in the Bible, "barren" would be right up there with "Golgotha." It was the demeaning adjective the seventeenth-century translators used to describe women who could not give birth. In an agrarian culture, "barren" described land that was unproductive or devoid of life, as bleak as the Middle Eastern wilderness through which the Israelites wandered on their way to the Promised Land. But the word can also serve as a metaphor for spiritual barrenness that is far more than a geographical wasteland or a gynecological condition.

"Barren" is the desolate description of people who cannot conceive of life the way God conceives it. I experience it as the:

- sterility of imagination in people who confine God's activity within the narrow limitations of their human intellect, resources, and powers;

- political frigidity of people who settle for this world with its economic injustice, racial inequity, political polarization, and self-destructive addiction to violence because they cannot imagine the fulfillment of God's vision of Shalom;

- dire diagnosis of our condition when we live as if there is no God to hear our prayers, to redeem our broken hearts, to rebuild our shattered lives, and to bring to birth otherwise-impossible possibilities.

Spiritual barrenness has more to do with what doesn't happen in the heart, mind, and soul than it does with what happens or doesn't happen in the womb. Any of us of any age can be spiritually barren. In fact, most of us experience it some of the time; some of us experience it most of the time.

"Don't be afraid, Zechariah. Your prayers have been heard."
(Luke 1:13)

Zechariah knew it was impossible for Elizabeth, whose womb had bypassed childbearing long ago, to conceive. Zechariah was just as old and "barren" as Elizabeth. It's no wonder he was "startled and overcome with fear" (Luke 1:12) when Gabriel showed up while he was on duty in the Temple. Zechariah might have been bored. Perhaps he served at the altar so often that it became a stale ritual with no capacity for surprise. He may have been so intensely focused on what he was doing that he was unaware of anything beyond himself.

I confess that as a pastor, I sometimes became so fixated on the mechanics of what we were doing in worship and how we were doing it that even the holiest of places became a barren place in which I was unaware of the presence of God. But I've also experienced those surprising moments when, like Isaiah in the Temple (Isa 6:1–8), I experienced with awe-stricken amazement an unmistakable awareness of the presence of something or someone beyond myself. Jacob was equally startled by a vision of a ladder connecting heaven and earth. Angels were going up and down on it like Christmas shoppers on a crowded department store escalator. He declared his surprise, "The Lord is definitely in this place, but I didn't know it" (Gen 28:16).

Surprising faithful people by fulfilling their long-held dreams or answering their most desperate hopes is evidently an essential part of the job description for angels. They show up when ordinary people least expect them with the invitation to become active participants in God's extraordinary work in the world. Each story contains its own peculiar and sometimes laugh-out-loud details, but the one thing they have in common is God made something happen that could not otherwise have happened.

Sarah, the matriarch of biblical faith, was as old and barren as Elizabeth. The promise that she would give birth was so outrageous that she laughed until her sides ached and tears flowed down her wrinkled cheeks. Abraham, her equally barren husband, laughed too. But God got the last laugh when the baby arrived and they named him Isaac, Hebrew for "laughter" (Gen 16:11; 17:19–20).

The same pregnancy-announcing angel brought the same astonishing promise to Manoah and his unnamed wife: "Although you are barren, having borne no children, you shall conceive and bear a son" (Judg 13:3). Against all odds, it happened! She conceived and bore a son named Samson, the athlete with the strong arms and the long hair.

The rabbis must have laughed out loud when they told the story of Hannah and the thickheaded men around her. Unable to conceive, she couldn't compete with Peninnah, the rival wife of Elkanah, who was birthing babies like rabbits and making fun of

Hannah with every delivery. Elkanah, with an exaggerated assurance of male importance, asked, "Aren't I worth more to you than ten sons?" Hannah didn't find that to be very helpful! Her prayers became so emotional that the old priest, Eli, with an equal dose of male insensitivity, assumed she had too much to drink. When he finally realized she wasn't drunk but desperate, he prayed that God would give her the child for which she was praying. To everyone's surprise, "The Lord remembered her . . . Hannah conceived and gave birth to a son" (1 Sam 1:1–20). In response, Hannah sang a revolutionary song of social change that Mary reprised when she and Elizabeth celebrated their equally impossible pregnancies (1 Sam 2:1–11; Luke 1:46–55).

The biblical stories of improbable pregnancies proclaim the way God barges into human history to invite ordinary people to participate in the fulfillment of God's redemptive purpose in ways that go beyond human power to conceive or control. These are not our predictable stories of a human journey toward God, but the unexpected stories of God coming to us, to do for us and through us that which we could never do for ourselves. Theologian and psychotherapist Ann Belford Ulanov confirmed, "We do not get to God from our side. . . . God is invading us as an event, invading human will and human imagination, rearranging all the ways we see and picture who we are, who others are, who God is." She said, "This invasion of power alters the entire force field in which we live, making a new creation of us, not a small change in direction."[1]

"How can I be sure of this?" (Luke 1:18)

Zechariah asked the obvious question, "How can I be sure of this? My wife and I are very old" (Luke 1:18). Gabriel seems to have lost patience with the old knucklehead. I imagine him speaking with angelic frustration, "Hey! Don't you know who I am? I'm Gabriel! I came straight from the presence of God to bring you some good news. But since you're too hardheaded to get the message, you're

---

1. Job and Shawchuck, *Guide to Prayer*, 132–33.

going to keep your mouth shut until it happens" (Luke 1:19–20, AP). Zechariah was left speechless (which might, of course, have been good news for Elizabeth!) until the baby arrived. That's when he rediscovered his voice and surprised everyone by naming the child John. Then he burst into a song predicting that his son would become the baptizer who announced the coming of the Messiah.

We'll miss the point of these pregnancy stories if we get hung up on gynecological explanations. These stories are more about faith than obstetrics. The possibility of Elizabeth's impossible pregnancy prepares us for the surprising promise that comes to Mary.

"God sent the angel Gabriel . . . to a virgin. . . . The virgin's name was Mary." (Luke 1:26–27)

The French phrase *le point vierge* translates as "the virgin point." It appears in the writings of the sixteenth-century mystic St. Teresa of Avila and the nineteenth-century writer St. Therese of Lisieux. In the twentieth century, Thomas Merton defined it as "that little point of nothingness and of *absolute poverty* [where we] meet God in a real and experiential contact."[2] He named it as "the final beginning, the definitive birth of a new creation. It is not the last gasp of exhausted possibilities, but the first taste of all that is beyond conceiving as actual."[3]

I experience *le point vierge* as any time or place where the Spirit of God does something in and through us that seems at least improbable, if not impossible. It's the point at which we accept our finite, human limitations and realize our spiritual barrenness. It's the disorienting moment when we know—in a way deeper than mere human knowledge—that God is working with and within us to accomplish God's purpose through us. The "virgin point" becomes the recurring time of decision when we say "yes" to the Spirit of God and allow the love of God that was born through Mary to be born again in and through our lives.

2. Bochen, *Thomas Merton*, 60–61, italics original.
3. McDonnell, *Thomas Merton Reader*, 367.

What About the Virgin Birth?

I interrupt Mary's story to offer a word about the virgin birth. I don't cross my fingers behind my back when I affirm the Apostles' Creed: "I believe in Jesus Christ, God's Son, our Lord, who was conceived by the Holy Spirit, born of the virgin Mary." I believe what the creed affirms about the uniqueness of Jesus, while not having a clue about the details of how it happened. It's a mystery, not in the sense of solving a British murder mystery, but in what Paul names as "the mystery hidden for ages in God who created all things" (Eph 3:9, NRSV). It's a mystery that is profoundly true in ways that are beyond our explanation but not beyond our experience. Frederick Buechner affirmed, "If you believe God was somehow in Christ, it shouldn't make much difference to you how he got there. . . . Life is complicated enough without confusing theology and gynecology."[4]

The virgin birth is the mystery of divine love in human flesh. Wesley historian and theologian Paul Chilcote wrote that John and Charles Wesley never attempted "to explain the incarnation in philosophical terms as if to master the inexplicable." Instead, they "simply described the lengths to which God's love will go to reach people wherever they are."[5] Charles Wesley's *Hymns for the Nativity of Our Lord* reverberates with awe-stricken amazement at the mystery of the God who came to be one with us, one of us.

> See in that Infant's face
> The depths of Deity,
> And labour while ye gaze
> To sound the mystery:
> In vain; ye angels, gaze no more,
> But fall, and silently adore.
> Unsearchable the love
> That hath the Saviour brought,
> The grace is far above
> Or man or angel's thought;

---

4. Buechner, *Wishful Thinking*, 94.
5. Chilcote, *Quest for Love Divine*, 100.

Bearing the Impossible Promise

Suffice for us, that God we know,
Our God is manifest below.[6]

I don't believe in Jesus because of the virgin birth; I believe in the virgin birth because of Jesus. I resonate with William Sloane Coffin's description of the incarnation as "the dazzling truth," which gradually dawned upon him.

> Jesus was both a mirror to humanity and a window to divinity, the most amount given to mortal eyes to see. God was not confined to Jesus, but, to Christians at least, essentially defined by Jesus. . . . What's finally important is less that Christ is Godlike but more that God is Christlike.[7]

The story of the child conceived in Mary's womb is the great mystery of the way the universal, self-giving love that is the essential character of God was present among us in a particular human body, in a particular place, at a particular time. It begins at *le point vierge* when Mary received a promise that the impossible would become possible through her.

"Look! You will conceive and give birth." (Luke 1:31)

I was born as the fulfillment of what appeared to be an improbable promise. My father was coming home from India at the end of World War II when he told his buddies that he and his wife would start their family with twin boys. We have no idea where he got that idea. All we know is that he announced it as the overly optimistic promise of an improbable possibility. And yet, no one was more surprised than my parents when it happened! In those pre-sonogram days, there was no warning that our mother was bearing twins. Labor was slow and my father was not permitted in the labor and delivery room. He was waiting at my grandparents' home near the hospital when the old-fashioned, wooden-boxed phone on the wall rang. The sudden delivery surprised everyone

---

6. Wesley, "Let Earth and Heaven Combine," lines 13–24.
7. Coffin, *Letters to Young Doubter*, 42.

including the family doctor who still made home visits with his black leather case in hand. He said, "Well, Ves, you got your twin boys!" Dad dropped the receiver the way a pop singer drops the mic at the end of a performance and ran to see the unexpected fulfillment of an unlikely promise. They had conceived something that seemed inconceivable and provided me with a living metaphor of the way a hopeful vision of the future is impregnated in the deepest womb of our imagination by the Spirit of God.

The entire history of human progress is driven forward by people who conceive what seems inconceivable; people through whom something that seems impossible becomes possible. Abraham Lincoln used the conception metaphor at Gettysburg when he reaffirmed the Founders' vision of "a new nation, *conceived* in Liberty, and dedicated to the proposition that all men are created equal." He said our bloody Civil War was "testing whether that nation, or any nation so *conceived* and so dedicated, can long endure."[8] We're still testing that well-conceived but still-unrealized proposition today.

The crucial word in what the Founders conceived is "all." E. Stanley Jones called it "the most explosive and revolutionary word in our national history."[9] The continuing tension in our nation is around who is included in "all." Anyone who thinks the equality conceived by our Founders has fully become flesh among us isn't paying attention! Sinister forces of white supremacy, sexism, homophobia, and anti-Semitism have slithered beneath the surface of our life together throughout our history. The persistent tension in our national body is our deeply imbedded resistance to birthing the promise our Founders conceived but that has not yet been fully delivered.

---

8. Lincoln, "Gettysburg Address."
9. Jones, *Christ of the American Road,* 66.

Bearing the Impossible Promise

"How can this be?" (Luke 1:34, NRSV)

Mary was flabbergasted by Gabriel's bewildering announcement. Her pubescent body had only recently become capable of pregnancy. She couldn't conceive of conception happening in her virgin womb. Like Zechariah, she asked the reasonable question, "How can this be?"

If we haven't asked the same question or if this story doesn't confuse or perplex us, we've either heard it so often that we are anesthetized to the surprise, or we've never really heard it at all.

Mary was just as confused as Elizabeth and Zechariah. So was Joseph. He's the "man in the shadows" of the birth narrative; a second-rate actor who only appears briefly on the stage, always the supporting character to the leading role played by Mary. When the fifteenth-century Italian artist Domenico Ghirlandaio painted his vision of the nativity, he positioned Joseph's head in the exact center of the canvas. Joseph stares up at a tiny, inconspicuous angel who flutters barely inside the upper, left-hand corner of the painting. And Joseph is scratching his forehead.

If scratching the head meant the same thing in the fifteenth century that it does today, I hear Joseph asking the same question Mary asked Gabriel. I suspect it's the question Mary "pondered in her heart" (Luke 2:19) throughout her life. If Ghirlandaio got it right, it makes room in the drama of the incarnation for every person who questions, doubts, or has a hard time believing a seemingly impossible promise can come true, but who chooses to participate in its fulfillment.

"The Holy Spirit will come upon you, and the power of the Most High will overshadow you." (Luke 1:35, NRSV)

It is, of course, physically impossible to conceive a child alone. Whether it occurs through sexual intercourse or by *in vitro* fertilization, when conception happens in a woman's body, it is not the result of something she does on her own. Someone else contributes to the creation of new life. In Mary's case (and metaphorically in our own), that someone is the Holy Spirit.

Luke described the work of the Spirit in Mary's life with the verb "overshadowed." The word brought to mind the Old Testament image of a mother bird hovering over her young (Deut 32:11). The "overshadowing" of the Holy Spirit carries us back to the creation story when "the earth was formless and empty . . . and the Spirit of God was hovering over the waters" (Gen 1:2, NIV). Charles Wesley called the Holy Spirit the "sacred energy" who conceives, creates, sustains, and recreates life.[10] The Spirit created the possibility of Mary's body becoming the body through which God's love becomes a breathing, bleeding reality among us.

Gabriel's answer to Mary's question was, "Nothing will be impossible with God" (Luke 1:37, NRSV). The same Spirit who first spoke creation out of chaos was doing it again, bringing new creation through Mary's body. It was an intrusive act of God that is beyond our power to conceive. What God did in Mary and wants to do in each of us is impossible without the Spirit who makes impossible things possible. But how does it happen? I resonate with Samuel Longfellow's experience of the Holy Spirit as truth, love, power and right.

> Holy Spirit, *Truth* divine,
> Dawn upon this soul of mine;
> Word of God and inward light
> Wake my spirit, clear my sight.
>
> Holy Spirit, *Love* divine,
> Glow within this heart of mine;
> Kindle every high desire;
> Perish self in Thy pure fire.
>
> Holy Spirit, *Pow'r* divine,
> Fill and nerve this will of mine;
> Grant that I may strongly live,
> Bravely bear, and nobly strive.

10. Young, *United Methodist Hymnal*, 88.

Holy Spirit, *Right* divine,
King within my conscience reign;
Be my Lord, and I shall be
Firmly bound, forever free.[11]

"Let it be with me, just as you have said." (Luke 1:38)

I'm encouraged by the way Luke holds together Mary's doubt with her commitment. She voiced the question that must have lingered with her until Pentecost, "How can this be?" With the same breath, she confirmed her obedience, "I belong to the Lord, body and soul, let it happen as you say" (Luke 1:38, Phillips). Strip away the spiritual sentimentality or mythical Mariology that has accumulated around Mary's story and we end up with a young girl who, with all her questions, doubts, and fears, said "yes." The impossible possibility would not have been possible without the presence and power of the Spirit of God, but it also would not have been possible without Mary's willing participation. It echoes the experience of Isaiah, who bore witness, "When I heard the Lord's voice saying, 'Whom should I send, and who will go for us?' I said, 'I'm here; send me'" (Isa 6:8).

A business marketing consultant underscored what every parent of a two-year-old toddler soon learns from their child. "It's easier for people to say no than to say yes to whatever you're asking them to do . . . because 'no' keeps them where they are with what they know (easy, familiar). Yes means having to do something new (hard)."[12] It would have been easier for Mary to tell Gabriel to go find another virgin. Saying "no" would leave her precisely where Gabriel found her as an innocent, ordinary girl in an ordinary, nowhere village. When Mary said "yes," she stepped away from a life that was familiar, predictable, and comfortable into a life that was strange, difficult, and unpredictable. But her "yes" became the way God's infinite love would become a finite reality in and through her.

11. Longfellow, "Holy Spirit, Truth Divine," italics added.
12. Wallace, "Saying No Is Easier," para. 1.

Surprised by Mary

Faithful people were surprised to discover how Mother Teresa wrestled with her faith. After her death, Father Brian Kolodiejchuk published the letters she wrote to her spiritual advisors across the years. The letters provided a narrative of years of utter desolation during which she struggled to hold together her doubts and her obedience. Kolodiejchik concluded, "There may have been many moments when her fidelity to her private vow was challenged, but with each new 'yes' she emerged more intimately united with the Lord to whom she was ready to give 'even life itself.'"[13]

I didn't experience the years of doubt Mother Teresa described. Neither do I expect to be canonized as a saint! But I have discovered that the way to new life always involves saying "yes." It means taking the next appropriate step in a growing obedience to the way of Christ. That kind of "virgin point" often comes to us as it came for Mary, at unanticipated times and in unexpected ways. One came to us on my forty-fifth birthday. Our bishop asked us to go from a place that was familiar, comfortable, and continually energizing, to a new appointment that turned out to be unpredictably challenging and unexpectedly difficult. We were given a choice. We could have said "no." But it felt like an unanticipated call from God. We accepted an irrational invitation to step into an unknowable future because it was where we sensed God was calling us to go.

I'm confident that if we had said "no," God would have continued to use us in the place where we were serving. But looking back three decades later, I thank God that we were given the opportunity and that with all our anxiety and doubt, we said "yes." The new thing we were called to do turned out to be a surprising gift as well as a difficult demand. That decision was *le point vierge* where we experienced the presence of the Spirit of God conceiving new possibilities in our lives and in our new congregation. (I told the story in *You Only Have to Die: Leading Your Congregation to New Life*.)

So, how does Mary, bearing the seemingly impossible promise of the birth of Jesus, become a spiritual metaphor for the way

---

13. Kolodiejchuk, *Mother Teresa*, 38.

the same seemingly impossible promise might be born in and through us?

Bearing a Child Changes a Woman's Body

Pregnancy is inescapably visceral. A new life takes up its own space in a woman's body. The child within the mother's womb gets in her way, reshapes her body, changes the way she eats, sleeps, walks, and thinks. A new body is being formed within her body and her body will never be the same.

Jerusha Matsen Neal underscores Luke's use of the Greek verb *bastazo*, meaning "to carry or bear." It appears again in Jesus' disturbingly direct warning, "Whoever doesn't carry [*bastazo*] their own cross and follow me cannot be my disciple" (Luke 14:27). Neal writes, "When the Spirit overshadows these followers of Christ, they carry a cross—or perhaps more accurately, they carry the Crucified One within them.... As with the work of bearing a child, they 'carry [*bastazo*] the marks' of that work in their bodies."[14]

"It's my cross to bear" has become a cultural idiom that can refer to just about anything unpleasant or difficult that is imposed upon us, from cancer to a grouchy neighbor, from economic disaster to a losing football team. But that's not the calling Jesus places before us.

Bearing the cross—bearing the crucified Christ in our bodies the way Mary bore Jesus in her body—is not primarily about the way I carry unpleasant burdens that are unwillingly imposed upon me, though it does reshape the way I respond to those experiences. Bearing the cross means choosing to live in ways that are consistent with the way Jesus lived, the words Jesus spoke, the kingdom of God Jesus promised, and the things Jesus did, all of which led him to the cross. It's the choice to take into myself a finite measure of the infinite love Jesus revealed, the pain he bore in his heart, the disappointment that caused him to weep over a city that did

---

14. Neal, *Overshadowed Preacher*, 119.

not know the things that make for peace (Luke 19:42), and the extravagant joy he shared with others.

Even as Mary chose to become the servant of the Lord in bearing this child, bearing the cross means saying "yes" to the invitation to take into my mind, heart, and soul some portion of Jesus' anger with the injustice and pain of a broken, sin-afflicted world. It involves taking action to repair the broken places and become an agent of God's reconciliation in Christ. It also means carrying within me his promise of new life.

Bearing the crucified Christ in my body took on a new and more disruptive meaning during the racial reckoning that was intensified by the murders of George Floyd, Ahmaud Arbery, and Breonna Taylor in the summer of 2020. It forced me to understand more clearly that I am the beneficiary of opportunities I inherited simply by being a white, straight, middle class, American male. None of the challenges I have faced were because I inherited darker skin, arrived on this side of the border as the child of undocumented workers, worshipped in a synagogue or mosque, or faced rejection because of my gender or sexual orientation.

I was called to break out of my comfortable, carefully insulated white bubble to learn from African American colleagues as they described their past and present experiences of racism; to feel the old pain and new hope of a gay pastor who chose to come out of the closet; to become more aware of the struggle of low-income workers who make the beds in upscale resorts but sleep in overcrowded, cheap motels on the outer edge of the Orlando theme parks; to sit with a son whose mother no longer knows his name as she drifts further away with Alzheimer's disease.

The magnitude of the world's pain and the minuteness of my heart also force me to recognize how much I can bear at any given moment and to practice the disciplines of prayer, solitude, friendship, and rest that can renew and strengthen me for the long haul.

Bearing a Child Realigns Relationships

Conception creates a new, life-changing relationship between the mother and the child being formed within her. It changes her relationships with others even as Elizabeth's and Mary's pregnancies changed their relationships with each other, their husbands, and the people surrounding them. Every pregnant woman experiences the sometimes beautiful and sometimes burdensome ways people relate to her the moment she walks through the door. One pregnant pastor asked why people think they can impulsively touch her obviously pregnant body!

In a similar way, bearing the crucified Christ in my body redefines my relationship with other people. Mary bearing Christ in her body becomes a living metaphor for the way I bear other people in my heart, mind, and soul. Paul defined this new relationship by calling followers of Christ to "bear one another's burdens" (Gal 6:2), to "[bear] with one another in love, making every effort to maintain the unity of the Spirit in the bond of peace" (Eph 4:1–3), and to "bear with one another . . . forgive each other; just as the Lord has forgiven you" (Col 3:13).

Rachel Held Evans wrote that, during her second pregnancy after a miscarriage, "as my skin stretched over my belly, it was as if it became more porous, more absorbent of the suffering of others."[15] When Christ is being born again in my body, my body is becoming the body of Christ in my interactions with other bodies. As the living Christ takes up residence in my body, my eyes see other bodies the way Jesus sees them; my ears hear the way Jesus would hear them. The love that became flesh in Jesus is progressively becoming a reality in my flesh as I bear with others in their joy and pain, their success and failure, their victory and defeat. I become increasingly more sensitive to the pain of injustice, the hurt of loss, and the courage of those who face it. I also experience the way others bear me and bear with me as a very finite human being who stands in need of the mercy, grace, and forgiveness that are ours through Christ.

15. Evans, *Inspired*, 45.

Surprised by Mary

Dietrich Bonhoeffer was writing out of his experience with students in his underground seminary when he described the way Christ calls his followers to bear and bear with each other.

> They must suffer and endure one another. . . . Bearing the burden of the other means tolerating the reality of the other's creation by God—affirming it, and in bearing with it, breaking through to delight in it. . . . Those who bear with others know that they themselves are being borne. . . . It is only in bearing with the other that the great grace of God becomes apparent.[16]

In his classic, *The Cost of Discipleship,* Bonhoeffer promised:

> Disciples will not be weakened by suffering, worn down, and embittered, until they are broken. Instead, they bear suffering by the power of him who supports them. The disciples bear the suffering laid upon them only by the power of him who bears all suffering on the cross. . . . They stand in communion with the Crucified.[17]

The good news is that when this kind of bearing seems utterly impossible, we are given real, flesh-and-blood people who show us the way. Some are history-shaping examples of Mary-like discipleship: Desmond Tutu, Mary McLeod Bethune, John Lewis, Dorothy Day, Mother Teresa, Pope Francis. But we've also been given saints whose names will never appear in historical records. I found them in every community I served. They are ordinary people who leave an extraordinary impression on our lives. They are burden-bearing people who listen with a Christ-like ear, offer faithful wisdom, and sustain our spirits along the way. We are born along by followers of Christ whose undeserved love, ruthless honesty, persistent faith, and exuberant joy not only bear us but enable us to bear others as well.

---

16. Bonhoeffer, *Life Together,* 100–3.
17. Bonhoeffer, *Discipleship,* 104.

Bearing a Child Renews Our Hope for the Future

Like a pregnant woman, we bear within our bodies the promise of the future and the pain of waiting for it. Before anyone could throw a baby shower, Mary headed off to visit her cousin Elizabeth. When she got there, she burst into song like a performer in a Broadway musical with words that reprised some of the themes of Hannah's song and placed her in the line of the Old Testament prophets.

> With all my heart I glorify the Lord!
>   In the depths of who I am I rejoice in God my savior.
> He has looked with favor on the low status of his servant.
>   Look! From now on, everyone will consider me highly favored
>   because the mighty one has done great things for me.
> Holy is his name.
>   He shows mercy to everyone,
>   from one generation to the next,
>   who honors him as God.
> He has shown strength with his arm.
>   He has scattered those with arrogant thoughts and proud inclinations.
>   He has pulled the powerful down from their thrones
>   and lifted up the lowly.
> He has filled the hungry with good things
>   and sent the rich away empty-handed.
> He has come to the aid of his servant Israel,
>   remembering his mercy,
>   just as he promised to our ancestors,
>   to Abraham and to Abraham's descendants forever.
> (Luke 1:46–55)

I've heard the Magnificat called "an aria of freedom," a "hymn of social protest," and a "song of liberation." It boldly announces the vision of life the way God intends it. I should not have been surprised to learn the military junta in Argentina banned public recitations of Mary's song in the 1970s when the Abuelas de Plaza de Mayo published it as their declaration of nonviolent opposition.[18] They were working to find and return their children and grandchildren who had disappeared. A decade later authorities in Guatemala banned it as well. They were following the nineteenth-century example of the East India Company who removed the Magnificat from the order for evening prayer.

We may be inspired by Mary's words, but we know how this weary world works; we know what our world tells us is and is not possible.

What are the odds that arrogant politicians will be scattered in the false pretense of their own greatness?

How likely is it that powerful people will be brought low, while ordinary, powerless folks are lifted up?

What chance is there, in a world where the rich keeping getting richer and the poor keep getting poorer, that the people with the least will be filled with good things while the wealthy go away empty-handed?

Mary's Spirit-impregnated vision carries us back to the Spirit-impregnated hopes of the Hebrew prophets, even as we look toward the day when the kingdoms of this earth really do become of the kingdom of God (Rev 11:15). Her singing touches deep places of our souls where we remember what God did in the past, are called to participate in what God is doing in the present, and hold onto the hope of what God will do in the future.

Here's the surprise: Mary sang as if what was promised had already come! Her bearing the Son of God created the possibility for something new, unexpected, and unpredictable to happen in her and through her for this world. God's yet-to-be realized kingdom was being formed in her. As she bore Christ in her womb, she dared to believe that she was participating in the fulfillment of God's promise right here, right now. That's hope!

William Sloane Coffin spoke in the spirit of the Magnificat when he described hope as "a state of mind independent of the state of the world. . . . Hope enables us to keep a steady eye on remote ends." He declared that hopeful people are "critical of the present

---

18. Abuelas, "History."

Bearing the Impossible Promise

only because they hold such a bright view of the future."[19] In an interview with NPR, the scholar, preacher, and social activist declared, "If your heart is full of hope, you can be persistent when you can't be optimistic. You can keep your faith despite the evidence, knowing that only in so doing does the evidence have any chance of changing. While I am not optimistic, I am always hopeful."[20]

Even when it's hard to be optimistic—which it often is!—Mary's song inspires us to be hopeful. Her words challenge us to live in ways that are consistent with the way revealed in Jesus. There's no need to wait! We can live now in ways that anticipate the way things will one day be. We can become part of the answer to our persistent prayer for God's kingdom to come and God's will to be done on earth as it is in heaven. We can live into that hope the way a pregnant woman bears the hope of the new life in her womb.

The district superintendent warned Donna Claycomb Sokol that her appointment to Mount Vernon Place United Methodist Church in Washington, DC, would be the hardest thing she had ever done and possibly the hardest thing she would ever do. The "glory days" when it was one of the largest Methodist churches in the nation with 4,500 members were fading memories gathering dust in a room filled with memorabilia. The congregation had dwindled to a handful of faithful folks who were older than Elizabeth and Zechariah. The lay leader was ninety and the finance committee chairperson was ninety-two. The grand old building that dominates an intersection in the heart of the city was in disrepair. Years of deferred maintenance left some spaces unusable. It was, by all the available evidence, a "barren" place.

Donna remembers, "I felt a remarkable pull to this place. I knew beyond a shadow of a doubt that God was calling me to guide a process of transformation that would allow a declining church to grow again."[21] She discovered the audacious hope of an impossible promise gestating deep in the soul of a dwindling congregation. Mabel Wright, the ninety-seven-year-old chair of the

---

19. Coffin, *Passion for the Possible*, 3.
20. Adler, "Peace Activist," para. 15.
21. Sokol and Owens, *New Day*, xiv.

Staff-Parish Relations Committee constantly reminded Donna, "Mount Vernon Place is in the center of Washington. Washington needs Mount Vernon Place, and Mount Vernon Place needs you. Don't you ever forget you have the best job in Washington."[22]

The church did not die. New life was conceived within it by the overshadowing presence of the Holy Spirit. Donna later reflected how she had grown and changed.

> I'm far more resilient than I thought I could be. I'm more dependent upon God and the strength and comfort found in my walk with Jesus than I have ever been before. . . . I know the power of friendships that not only endure, but grow stronger in changing seasons. . . . I continue to be amazed by how after 16.5 years, a full third of my life, I can still claim to have the best job in Washington as I serve alongside people I love, cherish, and respect in a city filled with so much potential for goodness and healing. . . . I am so thankful to still be standing, rejoicing, and longing to offer my all to every aspect of life.[23]

It still happens. Not in the gynecological way it happened in Mary's womb, but in the way the overshadowing presence of the Holy Spirit conceives within us what appears to be the impossible promise of the kingdom of God and empowers us to participate in the coming of that kingdom by bearing the crucified Christ in our bodies. Like Mary, we can become the ordinary people who bear the hope of an extraordinary promise which becomes possible by the power of the Spirit of God.

"Sing Me the Song Again, Mama"

Pastoral colleague, author, and friend, Magrey deVega imagined a very young Jesus asking his mother to tell again the story of the day the angel visited her and the song she sang with Elizabeth.

---

22. Personal correspondence.
23. Personal correspondence.

"Mama, tell me the story again of how the angel visited you."

"Well, dear, he caught me by surprise one day. He told me not to be afraid, and that God had chosen me to give birth to you."

"Were you afraid?"

"I was at first, of course. Nothing like this had ever happened to me, and I didn't know what others might think. But there was something about the presence of God in that angel that gave me great comfort. I said yes, and I'm so glad that I did."

"Why were you glad, Mama?"

"Because then I could have you in my life, dear! But more than that, I knew deep down in my heart that God was going to do great things to change the world, and that God wanted to do them through me. To exalt the humble, fill the hungry, remember the lowly: it is a privilege to be used by God in such a powerful way. We must say yes, even when it is difficult to do so. Do you understand, Jesus?"

"Yes, Mama. May I ask another question?"

"Of course, dear."

"Can you sing me that song again? The one you sang when you said yes to the angel?"[24]

Magrey hoped that years later, when Jesus was in the Garden of Gethsemane praying earnestly with a blood-soaked brow, the words and melody of his mother's song came back to his memory, giving him strength for the suffering ahead.

> In those moments when life is most difficult, and the pain and trauma of life have us in their grip, we often have our sharpest and clearest memories of the lessons our parents taught us about staying steadfast in our convictions and courageous in our actions. I think Jesus learned a thing or two about obedience from the woman whose obedience brought him into earthly existence.[25]

24. deVega, "How Jesus Learned Obedience," para. 7.
25. Personal correspondence.

2

Birthing the New Creation

"She gave birth to her firstborn child." (Luke 2:7)

"She gave birth." Luke could not have said it more simply. Mary's firstborn son arrived through the same process of labor and delivery by which every baby before or after has arrived. But everyone who has been in a delivery room (or watched *Call the Midwives* on PBS) knows there is nothing "simple" about it! That's why we call it "labor"! The biblical prophets never flinch at this. Jeremiah boldly compared the pain and fear his people felt to a woman in labor.

> I heard a cry, like a woman in labor,
>   a scream like a woman bearing her first child.
> It was the cry of Jerusalem gasping for breath,
>   stretching out her hand and saying,
> "I am doomed!
>   They are coming to kill me!" (Jer 4:31, GNT)

The birthing process is often long and painful. It always includes an element of risk and danger for both the child and the mother. Giving birth is physically exhausting and demands all the muscular strength a woman can give. Delivery is messy. No baby is born without water, blood, sweat, tears, and the discharge of the afterbirth when the placenta is released from the uterus. It's usually loud as the mother groans and screams the child into life.

And when the mother pushes the baby through the birth canal, there is an exhausted release that can only be called utter relief and sheer joy!

"The one who is born . . . will be called God's Son." (Luke 1:35)

As the early Christians looked back from this side of Jesus' life, death, and resurrection, they came to believe there was an unexpected uniqueness about this child. The birth stories were not an assumption with which they began but a conclusion to which they came. The apostles began in the book of Acts by proclaiming the cross and resurrection. Mark's gospel, the first to be written, focused on the cross with nothing to say about Jesus' birth or childhood. Luke and Matthew added the birth stories along with more of Jesus' teaching. Finally, John's gospel interpreted the story more theologically. Paul lifted words out of the worship of the ancient church to affirm that the one who was "in the form of God" humbled himself to be "born in human form" (Phil 2:5-8). J. B. Phillips paraphrased that affirmation to say, "He, who had always been God by nature, did not cling to his prerogatives as God's equal, but stripped himself of all privilege . . . being born as mortal man" (Phil 2:6-8, Phillips). Charles Wesley declared the mystery in one of his Advent hymns.

> Emptied of His majesty,
> Of His dazzling glories shorn,
> Being's Source begins to be,
> And God Himself is born![1]

Faithful people across the generations have tried to smother the uncomfortably visceral reality of Mary's labor and delivery with a heavy dose of syrupy spirituality. The second-century Gospel of James claimed that Mary gave birth without blood, sweat, and pain. St. Augustine (354–430) wrote that in both conceiving and giving birth, Mary was "all pure, without pain." (He should have checked that out with Monica, his mother!) The fourteenth-century mystic

1. Manskar, "Glory to God," para. 3.

Bridget of Sweden described Mary birthing Jesus as "miraculous materialization" in which her son appeared outside of her without going through her body. Despite these well-intended efforts, the Gospels tell the story in all its messy, painful simplicity. Rachel Marie Stone used the details of labor and delivery to carry us into the mystery of the incarnation.

> *A girl was in labor with God.* She groaned and sweated and arched her back, crying out for her deliverance and finally delivering God, God's head pressing on her cervix, emerging from her vagina, perhaps tearing her flesh a little; God the Son, her Son, covered in vernix and blood.[2]

The surprising simplicity of Luke's words, the visceral reality of giving birth, and the power of early Christian interpretations of it continue to haunt us with an unsettling question.

"How can this be?" (Luke 1:34)

Mary wasn't alone in asking, "How can this be?" Zechariah asked Gabriel the same question (Luke 1:18). Mary and Joseph's neighbors in Nazareth were still asking it thirty years later. The persistent gossip about the circumstances of Jesus' birth caused his hometown congregation to turn against him (Matt 13:54–58; Luke 4:16–30). Later, a man named Nicodemus asked the same question (John 3:1–21). He never knew Mary or heard her story, but his experience invites us to discover how the Christ who was born through Mary can be born again through us.

Nicodemus visited Jesus under the cover of darkness. He was a leader of the Pharisees, a teacher of the law, and a highly respected man in the community. He didn't want people to know he was hanging out with a no-name rabbi who said the kind of things Jesus said and stirred up trouble wherever he went. And yet, his intellectual curiosity and spiritual hunger drew him magnetically to Jesus.

---

2. Stone, *Birthing Hope*, 127, italics original.

Nicodemus reminds me of my young friend, Eric. During his senior year in college, he found himself asking, "Do I really want to become the person I'm on the path to becoming?" He told me, "That road didn't seem to hold any real hope, only emptiness." He visited a friend who listened deeply and joined him in multiple conversations. Eric testified, "Those conversations began to break down the wall I had built over the years. It was months before I was ready to commit to this faith, but I never would have started without those conversations."

I suspect Nicodemus had more than one surreptitious conversation with Jesus. It takes time to cut through the clutter of our lives to get to things that really matter. In those conversations, Jesus must have listened carefully as Nicodemus sorted through his deepest beliefs and uncovered his most unsettling doubts in search of a faith that made sense in his head and a difference in his heart.

Nicodemus's story was the designated text when I returned to preach at St. Luke's United Methodist Church, the congregation I helped birth in Orlando. The sermon would be part of a worship series in preparation for opening night of their production of *Oliver!*—the Broadway musical version of Charles Dickens's novel *Oliver Twist*. They asked me to compare Nicodemus to Fagin, the scheming pickpocket in the musical, when he sings, "I'm Reviewing the Situation."

You don't have to be a crook to identify with Fagin in that kind of a deeply personal review. He faces a typical midlife crisis when he wonders what will happen when he is seventy. (Some of us have already found the answer to that question!) He questions whether he will be able to get by on the money he's set by for retirement and wonders who will be with him in his final days. Nicodemus might have been wrestling with the same soul-level questions when he heard Jesus say, "Ye must be born again" (John 3:7, KJV).

"How can anyone be born after having grown old?" (John 3:4, NRSV)

The way some people talk about being "born again" tempts me to agree with the cynical comedian who said the problem with "born again" Christians is that they are twice as big a pain the second time around. But there's more going on in Jesus' words than can be captured in secular sarcasm or simplistic spirituality. Diana Butler Bass wrote:

> Few texts are more misquoted and misinterpreted than this selection from John—and few have been more widely influential. Since the First Great Awakening in the 1740s, it has been a key passage for evangelical Christians, usually quoted in revivals to convince "unbelievers" to be "born again."[3]

Like so many conversations in John's gospel, Jesus and Nicodemus talked past each other. The Greek word *anothen* can mean "born again," "born anew," and "born from above." The rest of the conversation confirms that Jesus was speaking metaphorically about being "born from above." But Nicodemus heard him saying "born again." As a result, Nicodemus missed the point of Jesus' metaphor.

- Jesus was talking about the Holy Spirit; Nicodemus was picturing an obstetrician.
- Jesus was describing the kingdom of God; Nicodemus was imagining maternity wards.
- Jesus was speaking metaphorically about being "born from above" or "born anew" but Nicodemus got hung up on being "born again."

Because Nicodemus took Jesus literally, he could not take Jesus seriously. His question was as honest as the question Mary asked Gabriel: "How is this possible?" The obvious answer is it's impossible. Even the Spirit of God cannot pop us back into the

---

3. Bass, "Sunday Musings," para. 2.

womb to be "born again." Jesus was describing a distinctive way of living that is not self-conceived. We can't make this up on our own.

Life in the kingdom of God is conceived and birthed within us by the Spirit of God. Paul called it a "new creation" in which our old way of living fades away and a new way of living comes into being (2 Cor 5:17). The "new creation" is the redemptive purpose of God revealed in Scripture being worked out in both our individual lives and through the sin-infected systems and social structures of our world. It's the prophetic promise of the way God intends this world to be, the vision God will accomplish at the end of time that is becoming a tangible reality among us now. It's nothing less than the life that was born into the world in Jesus being born into the world again through us. Though we cannot be born again, we can be born anew by being born from above.

We Can Be Born from Above into a New Way of Seeing

My wife and I remember the Christmas Eve when, after a very full day of preparations at home and multiple services at the church, we had settled in for "a long winter's nap." In the early hours of the morning, our four-year-old granddaughter crawled into our bed. We cuddled for a little while and then, with what I thought was grandfatherly wisdom, I said, "Julia, we can't get up until we see the sunshine in the window." I rolled over, closed my eyes, and expected her to follow my good example. A few minutes later, I felt a tap on my shoulder. I opened my eyes and Julia said, "Gampa, you can't see the sunshine with your eyes closed." She was correct!

Being born anew is the process by which our eyes are opened to see everything in our personal, relational, economic, and political life in the light of God's will and way revealed in Jesus. The Spirit enables us to see our prayer for the kingdom of God to come on earth being fulfilled in unexpected places through otherwise unnoticed and unrewarded disciples. We see it in faithful servants who follow the example of the man we call the "Good Samaritan." We see it in the relentless labor of faithful disciples who work to fulfill the vision of "liberty and justice for all" through unjust political and economic systems. We begin to see within the limited reality of what is the unlimited possibilities of what can be.

I preached the sermon comparing Fagin with Nicodemus forty-three years after the day we stepped onto the church property for the first time. But the Holy Spirit began birthing that congregation a decade before we arrived when the Orlando District of The United Methodist Church purchased an abandoned orange grove in the middle of nowhere. Some cautious committee members questioned the purchase, but others were "born from above" to a new way of seeing. They saw the unseen possibility of a day when a barren orange grove would become a vibrant outpost of the kingdom of God.

We Can Be Born from Above into a New Way of Loving

Nicodemus's conversation with Jesus sets the stage for John to announce the good news: "God so loved the world that he gave his only Son, so that everyone who believes in him won't perish but will have eternal life" (John 3:16). John's gospel also includes Jesus' final directive for his followers. "This is my commandment: love each other just as I have loved you" (John 15:12). The epistle named for John reiterates the same message. "If God loved us this way, we also ought to love each other.... If we love each other, God remains in us" (1 John 4:11–12).

The kingdom of God is the love that became flesh in Jesus becoming flesh again through us. The same Holy Spirit who enabled God's love to be born through Mary's body enables the same love of God to become a living, breathing, flesh-and-blood reality in the way we live. It doesn't happen in just one "born again" moment. It grows within us the way a baby grows in its mother's womb, enabling us, over time, to become the people God intends for us to be.

The decisive question is not whether I can name a specific date when I was "born again." It is not whether I believe precise doctrines, attend a particular church, or vote for a preferred candidate. The critical question is whether I am being continually born anew in loving God and loving others. Are the fruits of the Spirit

Paul named as "love, joy, peace, patience, kindness, goodness, faithfulness, gentleness, and self-control" (Gal 5:22–23) more alive in me today than they were yesterday? Am I more like Jesus today than I was last week or a month ago? Is the love that was born into the world through Mary's body being born again through me?

We Can Be Born from Above into a New Hope

The birth metaphor shows up again in the epistle named for Peter. "You have been born anew into a living hope through the resurrection of Jesus Christ from the dead" (1 Pet 1:3). Paul proclaimed the same "living hope" when he wrote, "We were saved in hope. If we see what we hope for, that isn't hope. Who hopes for what they already see? But if we hope for what we don't see, we wait for it with patience" (Rom 8:22–25).

People who are born from above demonstrate relentless hope in apparently hopeless situations. They hold onto the courageous hope that the kingdom of God that Jesus proclaimed is already present with us now and will one day be fulfilled in the whole creation.

The "living hope" the epistles affirm is:

- not only something we receive, but something we practice;
- not only something we feel, but something we do;
- not something that happens all at once, but something that grows over time.

I grew up hearing that being "born again" happened during drawn out "altar calls" accompanied with singing multiple verses of "Just as I Am." That's how we saw it happen in the Billy Graham crusades. I responded sincerely to many of those invitations at youth camps, revival services, and an old-fashioned Methodist camp meeting. Looking back, I cannot identify any one of those experiences as the specific moment I was "born again" but each of them set me in the direction of being "born anew." I learned that while being "born from above" can happen in decisive moments when we respond to the invitation to follow Jesus, being "born anew" takes a lifetime. We are continually being reborn as we grow. Dietrich Bonhoeffer taught his colleagues, "Christians will never feel that they have outgrown the place of their spiritual birth.... [They] are driven by the desire to receive it ever anew, to be born anew again and again."[4] He described the Christian's life as "a progression in us . . . from one degree of clarity to another, toward an ever-increasing perfection in the form and likeness of the image of the Son of God."[5]

The birthing process requires active participation by the woman giving birth. "Labor" means doing something! The birth narrative in Matthew includes the story of Joseph's participation through his obedience to the Holy Spirit. In Matthew, Joseph is consistently the subject of an active verb. He doesn't talk; he acts.

- "Joseph . . . *planned* to dismiss her quietly." (1:19)
- "When he had *resolved* to do this, an angel of the Lord appeared to him." (1:20)
- "He *did* as the angel of the Lord commanded him; he *took* her as his wife." (1:24)
- "Joseph *got up, took* the child and his mother, and *went* to Egypt." (2:14)
- "Joseph *got up, took* the child and his mother, and *went* to Israel." (2:21)
- "He *made* his home in a town called Nazareth." (2:23)

There's not a passive verb in the text. The only time Joseph speaks is when he obeys Gabriel by naming the newborn child Jesus (Matt 1:25). He takes Mary's child as his own, which meant that Jesus' life would define the rest of his life. In a similar way, birthing the new creation requires our active participation, too.

Paul's words to the Ephesians were drilled into my teenage memory from the King James Version: "For by grace are ye saved through faith; and that not of yourselves: it is the gift of God: Not

---

4. Bonhoeffer, *Sanctorum Communio*, 228.
5. Bonhoeffer, *Discipleship*, 286.

of works, lest any man should boast" (Eph 2:8-9, KJV). But just because the gift is "not of works" doesn't mean there isn't work for me to do. Paul also wrote: "Work out your own salvation with fear and trembling, for it is God who is at work in you, enabling you both to will and to work for his good pleasure" (Phil 2:12-13). E. Stanley Jones said we cannot "attain" our salvation by our own efforts; we cannot "retain" our salvation without personal and spiritual discipline.[6]

When baptized followers of Christ are received into membership in The United Methodist Church, they promise to "faithfully participate" through their prayers, presence, gifts, service, and witness. Prayerful study of Scripture, personal presence in worship and Christian community, generosity in sharing our wealth and our talents, energetic service in the world, and joyful witness to others are the time-tested practices by which we "faithfully participate" in birthing the new creation. Our behavior becomes the expression of what we believe. I've learned that some of us believe our way into new ways of behaving while others behave their way into a new way of believing.

We don't know when or how Nicodemus was "born anew." We do, however, see the change in Nicodemus's behavior. He was the only person who questioned the accusations the authorities threw at Jesus (John 7:50). At the end, he helped Joseph of Arimathea take Jesus' bloody, mangled body down from the cross. He provided spices for embalming, helped wrap the blood-soaked body in linen cloths, and laid it in Joseph's tomb (John 19:39-40). Nicodemus may have been the last human being to touch the human body to which Mary gave birth. Somewhere along the way, he was born anew.

---

6. Foster and Smith, *Devotional Classics*, 301-2.

Surprised by Mary

"I bring good news to you—wonderful, joyous news for all people." (Luke 2:10)

The end or goal toward which labor and delivery are moving is the "good news of great joy" (Luke 2:10, KJV) on the arrival of a new life. Jesus pointed to this end (which is always a new beginning) when he compared his disciples to a woman in labor. "When the child is born, she no longer remembers her distress because of her joy that a child has been born into the world" (John 18:20–21). It is the exuberant joy of being born into a new life as a parent.

I clearly remember leaving the hospital the day our first child was born. I was on my way to our two-room seminary apartment to share the good news with our family and friends when I was astonished with a sudden sense of surprise. People were walking along the sidewalks in Lexington, Kentucky, as if it were a normal day! Even the streetlights were changing as if nothing had happened! I felt an irrational urge to stop the traffic and announce the good news. Luke's birth stories reverberate with this kind of irrepressible joy.

- Elizabeth's child "leaped in her womb" when Mary arrived.
- Mary burst into singing the disruptive, hope-filled promise of social justice in the Magnificat. (Luke 1:46–55)
- The shepherds heard the whole creation resound in response to the announcement, "Don't be afraid! Look! I bring news to you—wonderful, joyous news for all people. Your savior is born today in David's city. He is Christ the Lord." (Luke 2:10–11)
- After their visit to Bethlehem, the shepherds "returned home, glorifying and praising God for all they had heard and seen." (Luke 2:20)
- The magi in Matthew's account "rejoiced with exceeding great joy" when the star led them to the house where Mary, Joseph, and the baby were staying. (Matt 2:10, KJV)

Christian people have been singing for joy ever since! We ended the Christmas Eve services in the congregations I served by singing "Joy to the World." Lowell Mason's familiar tune begins on the high D on the musical scale and descends a full octave on the first line. Then it lifts off again, carrying the singers' voices back up the scale to celebrate the joy that comes down to us and lifts us up again. When we lifted our candles above our heads on the last verse, the warm candlelight filled the darkened sanctuary as a bold witness to the light that defies every dark power and brings the death-defying promise of new birth to the whole world.

> He rules the world with truth and grace,
> And makes the nations prove
> The glories of His righteousness,
> And wonders of His love.[7]

Singing those words does not deny the undeniable fact that every evening is not Christmas Eve. Every night is not a silent night when all is calm and bright. We sing the song of joy in a dark world where the candle's light can easily be snuffed out by the winds of undeserved suffering, unexpected sorrow, and unrelenting injustice. If Jesus was born the same way we are born and into the same world in which we live, it means that Christ is born again into a world where every heart has not made him room and where nations do not yet prove God's righteousness. We are born anew into the same old world that does not yet know the wonders of his love. But despite any evidence to the contrary, we know, "The light shines in the darkness, and the darkness doesn't extinguish the light" (John 1:5).

Sadly, there's no song of joy for Fagin in the final pages of Dickens's novel or when the curtain falls on *Oliver!* But Dickens told us another story about a man who, after reviewing his situation by nighttime visits to his past, present, and future, was born from above and began living in a new way. His name was Ebenezer Scrooge. Here's the way Dickens described Scrooge's reborn life:

> Scrooge was better than his word. He did it all, and infinitely more. . . . He became as good a friend, as good a master, and as good a man, as the good old city knew, or

---

7. Young, *United Methodist Hymnal*, 246.

any other good old city, town, or borough, in the good old world. Some people laughed to see the alteration in him, but he let them laugh. . . . His own heart laughed: and that was quite enough for him. . . . It was always said of him, that he knew how to keep Christmas well. May that be truly said of us, and all of us![8]

It was always said of Vee Choate that she knew how to keep Christmas very well. She prepared for the season with the same grace-filled precision she employed to keep unruly groomsmen, anxious bridesmaids, and nervous brides in order as the church's wedding coordinator. She used the same precision to guide the pastors's schedules as our administrative assistant. She did it all with the joyful warmth with which she also directed the children's choir. Life was not always easy for her, but she radiated a relentless joy that was not dependent on circumstances. It percolated from a deeper place than happiness, leaving no doubt she was being born anew, again and again.

Vee decorated her apartment elaborately for Christmas. She hosted delightful parties and had a unique ability to find an equally unique gift for every person. She was shopping for last-minute gifts a week before Christmas when her car was broadsided in a busy intersection. She died in the ICU a day later.

My sermon in the memorial service acknowledged that speaking Vee's name and the word "death" in the same sentence felt like an oxymoron. Some of her friends said Christmas would be unbearable because of Vee's death. But the death-defying, good news of the gospel was that *only* Christmas could make Vee's death bearable. The birth of Mary's child proclaimed the good news that we can be born anew to eternal life. We ended the service by singing with defiant joy.[9]

> Good Christian friends, rejoice
> With heart and soul and voice;
> Now ye need not fear the grave;
> Jesus Christ was born to save!

8. Dickens, *Christmas Carol*, para 70.
9. Harnish, *All I Want for Christmas*, 33–35.

Calls you one and calls you all
To gain his everlasting hall.
Christ was born to save![10]

> *"Everyone who heard it was amazed at what the shepherds told them." (Luke 2:18)*

How long has it been since you were surprised by the Christmas story? A faithful congregation member said, "It must be difficult to come up with something new to preach on Christmas Eve. It's always the same story." I could honestly reply that I never faced that dilemma, not because there is so little to say, but because what needs to be said is beyond the ability of human language to contain. I discovered something that took me by surprise every year.

I've seen the nativity story performed in the splendor of the Radio City Music Hall Christmas Spectacular.[11] For more than two decades, I heard the gospel read by movie and television stars with massed choirs in the Candlelight Procession at Epcot Center. I lit the Christmas Eve candles in a small country church and in a town hall with a fledgling congregation that did not yet have a building. I sang the carols in a fast-growing community in the suburbs and a century-old church in the center of the city. I treasure the memory of each place. But it's hard to beat the way preschool-age children tell the story with angels in tinsel halos, shepherds in bathrobes, and wise men in Burger King crowns, particularly if one of those wise men is your three-year-old grandson!

The exhausted teachers were clearly ready for their Christmas break to begin. They were doing their best to keep things in order, but the production had its full share of children roaming around aimlessly, angel wings coming undone, and cardboard crowns slipping down in front of wise men's faces.

---

10. Young, *United Methodist Hymnal*, 224.
11. Harnish, *When God Comes Down*, 42–43.

Surprised by Mary

The little girl playing Mary was supposed to be standing in prayerful adoration beside the manger, but she noticed that the blanket around the plastic baby Jesus had come undone. She was totally oblivious of anything else that was going on when she picked up the baby and held him somewhat precariously in one arm while she took the blanket from the manger and spread it out on the floor. While the rest of the performance rolled on around her, she laid the baby down and wrapped the blanket perfectly around it.

No baby was ever more lovingly swaddled than this one! For her, that plastic baby might as well have been the real one who needed Mary to burp him. She placed plastic Jesus on her shoulder and patted his back while the rest of the children sang:

> Jesus, our brother, strong and good
> Was humbly born in a stable rude,
> And the friendly beasts around Him stood.
> Jesus, our brother, strong and good.[12]

My daughter was not the only parent or grandparent in the room who wiped a tear from her eye when Shelby, a five-year-old angel whose father and uncle were recently killed in a tragic automobile accident, announced Jesus' birth to the wiggling shepherds. She shouted with all the gusto a preschool girl could muster, "I bring you good news of a great joy. To you is born this day in the city of David a Savior who is Christ the Lord."

That's just how real this story is. The good news of great joy is proclaimed in a world where:

- parents of preschool children die in car accidents;
- pandemics disrupt the ordinary order of our lives;
- migrants spend cold nights on the streets of border cities;
- racism continues to infect relationships and systems around us.

The angels sing of "peace on earth and goodwill to all" in a world where:

---

12. Young, *United Methodist Hymnal*, 227.

Birthing the New Creation

- Herod still reigns;
- powerful nations still use violence to impose their will on weaker ones;
- manipulative politicians still spread lies and call it news;
- love still gets nailed to a cross by hate.

The Savior is born in a world where we all are like lost, confused shepherds who desperately need a Savior, whether we acknowledge it or not. The song of joy at this baby's birth is not the naïve denial of what the world has come to, but a courageous confidence in what has come to the world. The defiant joy echoes through the darkness the way people of Sarajevo heard the haunting sound of Albinoni's "Adagio in G Minor" when Vedran Smailović played his cello in the city's battle-scarred ruins during the 1992 siege. He returned to play every afternoon for twenty-two days, often under the threat of sniper fire. One reporter said the performance "seems frivolous in the face of such danger and bleak conditions, until [a person] witnesses his playing."[13]

The Christmas of 1864 was an equally war-torn time for Henry Wadsworth Longfellow. In 1861, his second wife died in a fire in their home. Longfellow was so severely burned in his attempt to rescue her he was unable to attend her funeral. In March 1863, his first-born son, eighteen-year-old Charles, signed up against his father's will to fight for the Union in the Civil War. In November, Charles was severely wounded in battle and was honorably discharged. The war was raging on Christmas Day in 1864 when Longfellow wrote his poem, "Christmas Bells." It was later set to music and became the Christmas carol, "I Heard the Bells on Christmas Day." Popular renditions usually leave out his painful description of war, which is as accurate in Ukraine today as it was in the United States back then.

> Then from each black, accursed mouth
> The cannon thundered in the South,

---

13. Murray, "Cellist of Sarajevo," para. 17.

> And with the sound
> The carols drowned
> Of peace on earth, good-will to men!
>
> It was as if an earthquake rent
> The hearth-stones of a continent,
> And made forlorn
> The households born
> Of peace on earth, good-will to men!

Longfellow named the despair we also experience.

> And in despair I bowed my head;
> "There is no peace on earth," I said:
> "For hate is strong,
> And mocks the song
> Of peace on earth, good-will to men!"

But the song of joy breaks through his despair with the clarity of church bells ringing on Christmas Day.

> Then pealed the bells more loud and deep:
> "God is not dead, nor doth He sleep;
> The Wrong shall fail,
> The Right prevail,
> With peace on earth, good-will to men."[14]

The most surprising part of the story is that we are born anew in order for Christ to be born again through us. Meister Eckhart wrote, "We are all meant to be mothers of God." Paul Vasile used Eckhart's words as the basis for a contemporary song:

> What good is it to me
> if Christ's eternal birth takes place unceasingly,
> but does not take place within me?
> What good is it to me
> for the Creator to give birth to a child
> if I do not give birth to him in my time and place.
>
> We are all meant to be mothers of God,
> for God is ever waiting to be born.

14. Longfellow, "I Heard the Bells on Christmas Day."

Birthing the New Creation

We are all meant to be mothers of God,
to give God a face, to give God a voice,
to give God a place in this world.

And so like Mary full grace,
we make our lives a welcome space.
We say yes to love in the midst of fear.
We say yes to hope, we trust that you are near.
We say yes to joy so deep it soothes the pain,
We say yes to peace and light and freedom once again.[15]

---

15. Vasile, "We Are All Meant."

3

Breaking the Heart

"Sorrow, like a sharp sword, will break your own heart."
(Luke 2:35, TEV)

No one expected this! Luke surprises us with an old man who announced an unexpected preview of what lies ahead for Mary. It isn't a pretty picture. I'm sure being the one through whom Christ was born had its full share of the joy Mary celebrated in the Magnificat. Jesus' use of humor suggests there was laughter around the Sabbath dinner table in Joseph's household. But Mary also experienced pain that would break her heart. Her story becomes a disturbing preview for every person through whom Christ is being born again. When the love of God that became flesh in Jesus becomes flesh in us, it will break our hearts.

"They brought Jesus up to Jerusalem to present him to the Lord."
(Luke 2:22)

Mary and Joseph obeyed the rules; they did what the Old Testament law required. They brought their son to the Temple to be circumcised eight days after his birth. That's when they named him Jesus, just the way the angel had instructed Joseph (Luke 2:21).

The name declared that the salvation hope, which animated the Hebrew faith in the past, was now alive in their child.

They returned to the Temple forty days after the birth for the dual rites of "redemption" of the first-born son and "purification" of the mother (Luke 2:22–24). The law called for the offering of a year-old lamb, but a couple of pigeons or turtle doves would suffice for parents who could not afford a lamb. That's what Mary and Joseph brought. It is an early sign of Luke's attention on poor and marginalized people throughout his gospel.

I suspect parents brought their babies to the Temple the way I watched young parents bring their children for baptism. Some took it seriously; others not so much. Some simply came because of family tradition, their baby in a flowing baptismal gown their families had worn for generations. I knew God would be faithful to the baptismal vows, but I wasn't sure they would be. Others came with genuine spiritual anticipation. They believed the Spirit of God continues to speak over the water the same words Jesus heard at his baptism, "You are my child, whom I dearly love" (Luke 3:22). They intended to live into the baptismal vow to "reject the evil powers of this world and accept the freedom and power God gives." They planned to "nurture this child in Christ's holy church."[1]

Mary and Joseph took the dedication seriously. They raised their son in the faith, recited the Scriptures, taught him to worship in the synagogue, and immersed him in the Hebrew tradition. Where else would Jesus have gotten it? The words he heard and the traditions his family practiced were so deeply embedded in his heart and mind that he instinctively drew wisdom and strength from them at every critical turning point in his life.[2]

"Simeon took Jesus in his arms and praised God." (Luke 2:28)

Mary and Joseph came with faithful expectation, but they never expected what happened. They were probably not the only parents

---

1. Young, *United Methodist Hymnal*, 40.

2. You can explore this subject more deeply in my book, *Finding Your Bearings: How Words that Guided Jesus through Crises Can Guide Us.*

bringing their babies to the temple that day. They might have been easily missed in the crowd. But Simeon was watching and waiting for this moment. He checked out each child in search of a baby boy who would fulfill the promise the Lord made to him a long time before. Some parents must have been uncomfortable with a strange, old, gray-haired man who peered over their shoulders or peeked under their baby blankets.

I imagine tears in Simeon's failing eyes when the Spirit led him to the child for whom he was waiting. This was the end of the line for him. He could die in peace. He shouted with all the passion his raspy voice could muster:

> Now, master, let your servant go in peace according to your word,
>   because my eyes have seen your salvation.
> You prepared this salvation in the presence of all peoples.
> It's a light for revelation to the Gentiles
>   and a glory for your people Israel. (Luke 2:29–32)

That was the good news! But there was more. I wonder if Simeon hesitated to go on as he looked into Mary's eyes and spoke words that cast a shadow over her joy with a prediction of pain.

> This boy is assigned to be the cause of the falling and rising of many in Israel and to be a sign that generates opposition so that the inner thoughts of many will be revealed. And a sword will pierce your innermost being, too. (Luke 2:34–35)

On one level, Simeon gave voice to a deeply human truth. It's inevitable. Sooner or later, a sword will pierce the heart of every parent because of something that happens to or is caused by their children. Being a parent or grandparent has its full share of joy, but it can also break our hearts. That's the painful truth the pastor doesn't announce while holding a squirming baby over the baptismal font and splashing some prayed-over water on the infant's head!

Before Mary could absorb the shock of Simeon's words, another senior citizen showed up. Anna was an eighty-four-year-old widow who was spending whatever time she had left on this earth worshipping God with fasting and prayer. She started shouting like a Spirit-intoxicated saint at a Pentecostal revival. She ran around the Temple as fast as her old legs could carry her, pointing out this baby to all the people who, like Simeon and Anna, were waiting for God's promise to be fulfilled. She was like the shepherds who told everyone they met what they had heard and seen in Bethlehem. As a result, "Everyone who heard it was amazed" (Luke 2:18).

We never hear from Simeon and Anna again. They would not live long enough to see what became of Mary's baby. Like them, we may not live long enough to see the results of the work we've done in obedience to Christ or the difference we've made in another person's life. But John Wesley used Simeon and Anna to offer a word to senior citizens "whose hoary heads, like theirs, are a crown of glory." He challenged us "to labor to leave behind those to whom Christ will be as precious as he has been to them; and who will be waiting for God's salvation, when they are gone to enjoy it."[3] All of us, of any age, have work to do in passing the faith on to the next generation. As the old saying goes, we plant trees under which other people will sit. Any one of us can use the strength, wisdom, and experience we have gained to plant seeds of truth, justice, and compassion in our church and community. Like Simeon and Anna, we can practice the spiritual disciplines that will enable us to see the love of God at work around us. We're never too old to bear witness to the hope we find in Jesus Christ.

When Mary and Joseph "completed everything required by the Law of the Lord" they headed back home to Nazareth, no doubt still in shock from what they had experienced. Luke summarized Jesus' entire childhood in one verse, "The child grew up and became strong. He was filled with wisdom, and God's favor was on him" (Luke 2:39–40). Matthew, however, inserts a disturbing story Luke either had not heard or could not bring himself to tell. I'd like to leave it out, but it's in the gospel and it's still alive among us.

---

3. Wesley, *Wesley's Notes*, para. 38.

Surprised by Mary

"A voice was heard in Ramah." (Matt 2:18)

It's no surprise that King Herod was "troubled" when mysterious visitors from the East arrived in Jerusalem in search of a newborn king (Matt 2:1–12). The more troubled he was, the more troubling he became. There was only room for one king in Israel and it was Herod! He didn't hesitate to get rid of anyone who got in his way. His instinctive reaction was to lie. He told the magi, "Go and search carefully for the child. When you've found him, report to me so that I too may go and honor him" (Matt 2:8).

The Spirit-led magi knew a con artist when they met one. They tricked the trickster and took another route home. Their quick double-cross threw Herod into a tyrannical rage. He ordered his stormtroopers to slaughter all the boys under two years old in Bethlehem. Matthew quoted the prophet Jeremiah to describe the grief of the parents in Bethlehem.

> A voice was heard in Ramah,
>   weeping and much grieving.
>   Rachel weeping for her children,
>   and she did not want to be comforted,
>   because they were no more.
> (Matt 2:18; Jer 31:15)

What's Rachel doing here? Why did Matthew insert her into the story? Faithful readers of Torah remembered Rachel as Jacob's beloved wife who, after long years of infertility, gave birth to Joseph. They were near Bethlehem when she died giving birth to Benjamin. Jacob expressed his grief by setting up a pillar on her grave (Gen 35:19–20). Generations later, Jeremiah heard Rachel's voice in the weeping of the Israelites as they passed her grave on their way into exile in Babylon, not unlike the Cherokee people along the Trail of Tears. Matthew used Jeremiah's words to name the grief in the broken hearts of parents who face the death of a child, particularly children who die in the brutal violence of our world, whether they are in Bethlehem, Sandy Hook, Parkland, or Uvalde.

The crying would have broken Mary's heart if she had been there to hear it. Gabriel warned Joseph to get out of town to escape Herod's maniacal wrath. They became political refugees in Egypt, like modern-day refugees escaping from Ukraine.

Why did Matthew tag this ghastly account to the end of the birth story? For one reason, this gospel was written primarily for a Hebrew community. It identified Jesus as the fulfillment of the messianic hope of the Old Testament prophets. People who knew the stories from their history could hear a subtle comparison between Jesus and Moses. Both were born when the covenant people were oppressed by foreign powers: Egypt and Rome. Both of their lives were threatened by powerful rulers: Pharoah and Herod.

The story is also here because the central theme of Matthew's gospel is the kingdom of God revealed in Jesus. Matthew framed Jesus' life between two ruthless political rulers: Herod at his birth and Pilate at his death. They represent the persistent tension between the kingdoms of this world and the kingdom of God. God's kingdom comes and God's will is done in the tension of our politically conflicted, sin-distorted, and power-hungry world.

Matthew disrupts our Christmas nostalgia to bring us to face the suffering, injustice, fear, and death that result from political and economic systems that function in opposition to the reign and rule of God. The Bible never shrinks from the ugly truth about who we are as broken people living in a broken world—a world in which God's kingdom has not yet fully come and God's will is not always done. The Psalms are ruthlessly honest about the pain we feel and the frustrations we face. The Prophets offer hope without silencing our tears in a smothering blanket of shallow spirituality. Jesus calls us to follow him on the costly way of discipleship that always leads to a cross. Herod's world is the world into which every child is born.

As I write these words, we can see Herod's murderous wrath repeating itself in Putin's invasion of Ukraine. *The New York Times* journalist Oleksandr Chubkoc named "the reality—the randomness of death, the often life-changing violence and suffering visited in one terrible moment." He could have been describing Bethlehem when he wrote, "The small riverside community seemed an undeserving, even senseless, target. . . . But, perhaps, in this brutal war of indiscriminate Russian violence, that was precisely the point."[4]

If Christ is being born again through us the way he was born through Mary, the sword that pierced her heart will pierce our hearts as well. The closer we walk with Christ, the more deeply we feel the brokenness of this world. We will hear the weeping in Bethlehem in bombed-out homes in Ukraine and the all-too-common gun deaths in our communities. We will see the anxiety of the Holy Family fleeing to Egypt in the faces of families who risk their lives to escape to our southern border. We find the infant Mary cradled in her arms, in the arms of parents in refugee camps in Poland or sleeping on the streets in El Paso.

Ultimately, however, Herod's way never works. Matthew lifted the light of hope when he wrote, "After King Herod died . . ." (Matt 2:19). The same angel who told Joseph to take Mary as his wife and to escape to Egypt now tells him to return to Israel. Herod had his day. Like every autocratic ruler then and now, Herod "struts and frets his hour upon the stage / And then is heard no more."[5] But Jesus came back! The cruelty and injustice of this world cannot ultimately destroy or deny the relentless strength of the infinite love that became flesh through Mary. But for Mary, this was just the beginning of Simeon's painful prediction.

"Child, why have you treated us like this?" (Luke 2:48)

Being Jesus' mother could not have been easy. Parenting never is! Her son's childhood was evidently so much like every other little boy in Nazareth that Luke found nothing extraordinary to tell. A beloved Christmas carol simply affirms:

> Jesus is our childhood's pattern;
> Day by day, like us He grew;
> He was little, weak and helpless,

---

4. Chubkoc, "Russian Missile," para. 18.
5. Shakespeare, *Macbeth,* act 5, scene 5, line 28.

Breaking the Heart

Tears and smiles like us he knew.[6]

But through the ordinary joys and frustrations of parenthood, the extraordinary memory of Simeon's disturbing prediction must have haunted Mary's soul. She would have experienced moments when the reminder of who Jesus was and what he would become took her by surprise. One of those surprises happened when Jesus was twelve years old. Like every teenager entering adolescence, he was sorting out who he was and what he would do with his life.

Mary and Joseph joined their relatives and friends on the annual Passover pilgrimage from Nazareth to Jerusalem "according to their custom" (Luke 2:42). Nothing unusual happened until they headed home. No one could find Jesus! Every parent can imagine their frantic fear as they searched for him for three days. They finally found him with the teachers in the temple who were "amazed by his understanding and his answers" (Luke 2:48). Eugene Peterson captured the very real, human emotion of the encounter in his paraphrase.

> His parents were not impressed; they were upset and hurt. His mother said, "Young man, why have you done this to us? Your father and I have been half out of our minds looking for you." (Luke 2:48–50, MSG)

Jesus' reply was enough to break his mother's heart. "Why were you looking for me? Didn't you know that I had to be here, dealing with the things of my Father?" I suspect Joseph was ready to tell Jesus not to talk back to his mother that way! Luke explained, "They had no idea what he was talking about" (Luke 2:48–50, MSG).

Perhaps they had no idea, though that's a little hard for me to accept given everything Luke has already told us. Perhaps they didn't understand. Or perhaps they didn't *want* to understand. Perhaps they weren't sure they wanted their son to fulfill Simeon's prediction. If so, their problem could be ours as well. It's generally not what we don't understand in the Bible that gives us trouble. Our problem is often with things we understand all too clearly but don't want to obey. We know the way Jesus is calling us to go but

---

6. Young, *United Methodist Hymnal*, 250.

we don't want to follow. Perhaps we are afraid that we will end up with a broken heart.

The Gospels go silent for about twenty years. But Mary's life isn't any easier when we pick up her story. It must have broken her heart when:

- Her neighbors rejected Jesus' message in the synagogue, ran him out of town, and tried to throw him off a cliff. (Luke 4:16–30)
- She told Jesus they ran out of wine at the wedding in Cana and he reacted with what feels like a condescending question, "Woman, what does that have to do with me?" (John 2:3)
- Someone in the crowd told Jesus his mother and brothers were outside waiting to see him. Jesus responded, "Who is my mother? Who are my brothers?" It didn't help when he continued, "Whoever does the will of my Father who is in heaven is my brother, sister, and mother." (Mark 3:32–35)
- Jesus' siblings wanted to take him home because they thought he was out of his mind. (Mark 3:21)
- She stood beside a Roman cross and watched her son suffer and die. (John 19:25)

Each heartbreaking surprise reminded Mary of Simeon's disconcerting warning and of where her initial "yes" to Gabriel's invitation would inevitably lead. When we allow Mary's story to become our story, we discover that becoming the people through whom Christ is born again means allowing the love that pierced her innermost being to pierce our lives as well.

Old Testament scholar Ellen F. Davis was commenting on David's heartbroken prayer in Psalm 51 when she wrote, "Willfully letting your heart break and then offering the pieces to God is a radically counter-cultural idea." She concluded, "It is only broken hearts that are truly open toward God." She called this spiritual discipline "voluntary heartbreak."[7] Why would any of us, in our self-indulgent, self-protecting, selfie-addicted culture, willfully let

---

7. Davis, *Getting Involved with God*, 168–69.

our hearts be broken? What will it mean for us to allow the sword that pierced Mary's inner being to pierce our souls as well?

A Broken Heart Opens Our Lives to Share the Pain of Others

I was a seminary student when I made my first pilgrimage to the Trappist monastery near Bardstown, Kentucky. We joined the monks in the darkening shadows of the sanctuary for Compline, the last service of the day. The focal point was the candle-lit icon of Mary cradling the Christ child in her arms. When the monks chanted, "Hail, Holy Queen, Mother of mercy, turn your eyes of mercy toward us," I remembered the way my mother sang to us as she tucked her children into bed. I realized that one of the reasons faithful people have historically turned to Mary is the feeling of security and comfort people found in her as their spiritual mother. When their hearts were broken, they turned to the one whose heart had been broken before theirs.

I learned to be a more loving pastor and a more Christ-like person when I allowed the sword that pierced someone else's heart to pierce my heart as well. I remember the faces and hear the voices of people whose cries were not silenced by pastoral platitudes:

- friends whose teenage son died in a violent car accident;
- four young boys who were robbed of their father by cancer;
- a faithful mother who opened her heart to accept her gay son;
- parents who struggled to save their child from drug addiction;
- an attorney who lost his job because he told the truth;
- a young man whose call to ministry was rejected because of his sexual orientation;
- spouses who held the hand of their long-time partners as they took their last breaths.

They taught me what it means for our hearts to be "broken open rather than broken apart."[8] They continue to remind me that when our hearts break with our awareness of what breaks the hearts of others, we become more aware of things that break the heart of God.

A Broken Heart Forces Us to Confront the Reality of Sin

Karl Menninger caused a stir fifty years ago when he published *Whatever Became of Sin?* While specific situations he named have changed, the question he asked still haunts our spiritual complacency. Menninger was consistent with Scripture when he diagnosed the ailment ("sin") as our radical selfishness, which results in destructive behaviors ("sins") that harm both ourselves and others. His prescription was: "Caring. Relinquishing the sin of indifference." He promised, "If the concept of personal responsibility and answerability for ourselves and for others were to return to common acceptance, hope would return to the world with it."[9] So, what about sin?

A woman who read the first draft of this chapter asked a question I had not directly considered, but which underlies the purpose of this book: Was Mary without sin?

Growing up with the Immaculate Conception Roman Catholic Church near the center of our town, I thought the term referred to the conception of Jesus. I was doing research for this book when I learned it refers to Mary. Belief that Mary was free from original sin began as early Christian tradition but did not become official Roman Catholic doctrine until 1845. As a Protestant, I agree with preacher and professor Jason Byassee who wrote, "It is Mary's ordinariness that keeps the incarnation scandalous, not her sinlessness. That God is born in the midst of a quite average life is the claim Mary safeguards."[10]

---

8. Palmer, *On the Brink*, 49.
9. Menninger, *Whatever Became of Sin?*, 188–89.
10. Byassee, "What about Mary?," para. 14.

"Mary's ordinariness" is a basic conviction I bring to this book. The extraordinary affirmation that Christ was born through an ordinary woman is our hope that Christ can also be born in us. If I am required to be without sin before Christ is formed in me, there's no possibility that Paul's impregnating prayer for Christ to be born in me can be fulfilled. In fact, when Christ is being born in me, I become more aware of my brokenness, failure, and sin. As the Christ who became flesh through an ordinary young woman in Nazareth becomes flesh in me, my heart will be broken by the ordinary ways this world and my life within it are twisted, infected, damaged, and broken by sin.

Like many pastors of my generation, I questioned the value of written prayers of confession in worship. We learned in church growth workshops that it was more effective to draw people with a positive word about how good we can be rather than reminding them of how bad we are. We doubted the integrity of asking people to recite words they didn't believe. But looking back, I wonder if our well-intended efforts were a subtle denial of our need to name our complicity in the sin in our lives and the brokenness in our world. The traditional Prayer of Confession probes into the dark corners of our hearts and our behaviors.

> Merciful God,
> we confess that we have not loved you with our whole hearts.
> We have failed to be an obedient church.
> We have not done your will,
> we have broken your law,
> we have rebelled against your love,
> we have not loved our neighbors,
> and we have not heard the cry of the needy.
> Forgive us, we pray.
> Free us for joyful obedience,
> through Jesus Christ our Lord. Amen.[11]

A well-crafted prayer of confession in worship or in our personal quiet time can remind us that there is such a thing as sin, and

---

11. Young, *United Methodist Hymnal*, 8.

we are involved in it. A prayer like Psalm 51 can awaken us to broken places we would otherwise avoid or deny. If none of the words fit today, they're sure to fit someday! If we can't name anything that needs to be confessed, healed, or restored, we risk confirming the warning in the epistle of John, "If we claim that we're free of sin, we're only fooling ourselves" (1 John 1:8, MSG). David stopped fooling himself. He confessed his sin with courageous honesty.

> I know my wrongdoings,
>   my sin is always right in front of me.
> I've sinned against you—you alone.
>   I've committed evil in your sight. (Ps 51:3–4)

The epistle continues, "If we admit our sins—simply come clean about them—he won't let us down; he'll be true to himself. He'll forgive our sins and purge us of all wrongdoing" (1 John 1:8-9, MSG). Ellen Davis promised, "When we let our hearts break before God, the pieces do not sink into oblivion. They are borne up, they float, yes, they sail on the tide of God's mercy."[12] Psalm 32 (perhaps also from David) expresses our need for confession and the mercy that follows it.

> When I kept quiet, my bones wore out;
>   I was groaning all day long—
>   every day, every night!—
> . . .
> So I admitted my sin to you;
>   I didn't conceal my guilt.
>   "I'll confess my sins to the Lord," is what I said.
>   Then you removed the guilt of my sin. (Ps 32:3–5)

I question whether Mary was sinless, but I know I'm not! And I know I stand in need of God's mercy and of the means of grace the church provides, particularly in the sacrament of holy communion.

---

12. Davis, *Getting Involved with God,* 170.

Breaking the Heart

A Broken Heart Creates Space for God's Mercy

At the beginning of Luke's gospel, the pregnant Mary rejoices in the tangible ways God "shows mercy to everyone, from one generation to the next" (Luke 1:50). Zechariah celebrated the promise of God's mercy in anticipation of John's birth:

> By the tender mercy of our God,
>   the dawn from on high will break upon us,
> to give light to those who sit in darkness and in the shadow of death,
>   to guide our feet into the way of peace.
> (Luke 1:78–79, NRSV)

Oscar Wilde, the flamboyant nineteenth-century Irish poet and playwright, was sentenced to two years of hard labor for homosexual behavior. He never recovered physically and spent his final years in exile in France where he died at the age of forty-six. His last work was the epic poem "The Ballad of Reading Gaol," which painted a vivid picture of the inhumane conditions of nineteenth-century English prisons. But he included a word of hope for our broken hearts.

> Ah! happy day they whose hearts can break
> And peace of pardon win!
> How else may man make straight his plan
> And cleanse his soul from Sin?
> How else but through a broken heart
> May Lord Christ enter in?[13]

When our hearts are broken, the broken places create space for God's mercy to enter in. How else can Christ find a place to be born again in the otherwise crowded and noisy complacency of our comfortable lives?

A balustrade with classically designed, evenly spaced concrete posts stretches for six miles along the sidewalk on Tampa's Bayshore Boulevard. Early one morning, my walking partner noticed the sunlight casting evenly spaced shadows on the sidewalk.

---

13. Wilde, "Ballad of Reading Gaol," part 5, stanza 14.

He quoted a legal principle that comes from the nineteenth-century English jurist Sir Henry James Sumner Maine, "Substance is gradually secreted through the interstices of process."[14]

The word "interstices" surprised me. They are gaps between closely spaced objects like the pillars in the balustrade. They are the empty spaces that allow something we didn't expect to seep through our orderly patterns of behavior. The sixteenth-century priest and mystic St. John of the Cross said God "keeps the interstices / In our knowledge, the darkness / Between stars."[15]

Sometimes God's mercy breaks into our lives with the silent explosion of sunlight breaking through a cloudy sky. That happened for three of the disciples who saw Jesus transfigured on the mountain (Matt 17:1–9). But everyone else experienced the same transfiguring presence when they came down from the mountain and Jesus healed an epileptic boy no one else could help (Matt 17:14–21).

I thank God for every transfiguring, "mountain top" experience in my life. We need surprising times of spiritual awakening. But more often, we experience God's mercy in the interstices, the intervening spaces between the transfiguring moments in the gospel story and in our own experience. God's grace secretes into our lives through cracks in the façade of our own goodness or fissures in our self-absorption. Christ's love seeps into our experience through the silent spaces in the ordinary patterns of our spiritual discipline.

A Broken Heart Is a Burden We Share

It was July 26, 1979. One of the pioneer members of the new congregation we were birthing in Orlando asked me to pray for her friends, a United Methodist pastor named Tom Price and his wife, Amaryllis. Their twenty-one-year-old son, Richard, died by gunfire in Washington, DC. It was one of those random acts of violence that happens all too often in our overly armed, violence-addicted

---

14. Maine, *Dissertations*, 390.
15. Peterson, *Christ Plays*, 156.

country. The handful of folks in our fledging community opened their hearts to share the heartbreak of our fellow church member and her friends.

Two months later, on September 11, 1979, the Price's phone rang again. Their second son, eighteen-year-old David, was in an intensive care unit as the result of a tragic car accident. He died ten days later. Two sons in two months, lost in sudden and senseless death. The heartbreak seemed as unbearable as it was unimaginable. But sharing their heartbreak taught us to "bear one another's burden" (Gal 6:2). It also created a connection that has lasted across the decades.

I asked the Prices to share how they navigated the years following their sons's deaths. Amaryllis wrote:

> Our loss is always there. All of us are more compassionate and more eager to reach out to others. I treasure people in my life unbearably. Amazing experiences connected to the boys have come all along the way, though none as wonderful as having them with us now.

Tom reflected:

> Their deaths put me closer to suffering humanity, a sense I might not have known had this not happened to us. I am more sensitive to the fragility of life, the crucial importance of relationships, and the ties that bind us to family and friends. Without our loss, I might have taken it all for granted.

He also affirmed the strength that came from knowing that other hearts were breaking along with theirs:

> We did not bear our loss in isolation. We were members of a community. I remember saying that I could not even stand up without the support of all those around me. The community support was so strong that after Rick's funeral, we felt refreshed. After David's death, there was no comfort, only the strength of faith to put one foot in front of the other.[16]

16. Personal correspondence.

Surprised by Mary

A Broken Heart Can Become a Source of Healing

You don't need to be a Roman Catholic to identify with the prayer:

> Immaculate Heart of Mary, please touch our wounded and broken hearts, and present them to the wounded Heart of Jesus, so that our wounds will be healed. Amen.

The longing of every sword-pierced heart is that, by God's grace, our wounded hearts will be healed and that we will become the agents of that healing for others.

I had not seen the news when Bishop Gregory Palmer met me at the airport in Columbus, Ohio. A Somali man drove over the curb on the Ohio State University campus, plowed into a group of students, jumped out of his car, and attacked people with a butcher's knife, injuring eleven people. Police shot the driver who died on the street. The authorities had not determined a reason for his attack. It had, however, heightened the anxiety of people in the Muslim community. Bishop Palmer took me along to a gathering of church and community leaders at Maynard Avenue United Methodist Church.

We met the imam who was providing care for the family of the attacker. He said, "We aspire to inspire until we expire." A Muslim woman who led a community outreach program for young adults wept as she wondered what they might have done to help the young man. A United Methodist woman said the Spirit led her several weeks earlier to reach out in friendship to the Muslim community. She contacted the local mosque. They put her in touch with one of their families. She invited them to dinner at her home. The Muslim family returned the invitation. They were already planning a Muslim / Methodist potluck supper. They were finding healing for their broken hearts by becoming a gift of healing for their community.

I am writing in the aftermath of another school shooting. Three children died in another of our uniquely American occurrences growing out of our uniquely American addiction to guns. We know the way it goes. Again, our hearts are broken, although it happens so often that we risk becoming immune to the headlines.

Again, we mourn. Again, we pray. And again, too many of our politicians at every level of our government call for "thoughts and prayers" but refuse to take any action that might reduce the increasing number of families, communities, and congregations whose lives are forever impacted by the loss.

But this time, the chaplain of the Senate, retired Rear Adm. Barry C. Black, had the courage and faith to pray on the floor of the Senate, "Lord, when babies die at a church school, it is time for us to move beyond thoughts and prayers." He asked God to "remind our lawmakers of the words of the British statesman Edmund Burke: 'All that is necessary for evil to triumph is for good people to do nothing.'" He concluded with this petition, "Lord, deliver our Senators from the paralysis of analysis that waits for the miraculous. Use them to battle the demonic forces that seek to engulf us."[17]

If I were still a pastor leading worship, I hope I would have the courage to pray that prayer and the faith to believe it could make a difference. And every time this kind of tragedy happens, there are people who rise from their tears, leave their "thoughts and prayers" behind, and go to work to make a difference about the gun violence in their community.

A Broken Heart Can Become the Crucible for Joy

C. S. Lewis bore witness to one of the most profound mysteries of the faith when he titled his spiritual autobiography *Surprised by Joy*. An unexpected joy surprises followers of Christ who willingly allow their hearts to break. It is joy that is deeper than happiness and stronger than tears, joy that is refined and purified in the crucible of pain.

The writer of Proverbs described the process with a powerful metaphor, "As silver in a crucible and gold in a pan, so our lives are refined by God" (Prov 17:3, MSG). Like the crucible in which molten steel is prepared, or the fire in which gold and silver are

---

17. Wang, "Senate Chaplain," paras. 3–4.

tested, the hollow place in our broken hearts is the space in which God's love can refine our pain and open our lives to joy. When nothing else matters, we discover what really matters most if we are open to discovering it. Some people, sadly, go into the fire and come out with harder hearts—hearts that are impervious to the pain of others and insensitive to the Spirit of Christ. But those who are open to receiving it discover what Charles Wesley meant when he taught us to pray:

> Oh, that in me the sacred fire
> Might now begin to glow,
> Burn up the dross of base desire,
> And make the mountains flow!
>
> Refining fire, go through my heart,
> Illuminate my soul;
> Scatter thy life through every part,
> And sanctify the whole.[18]

Looking back on the immeasurable loss of their sons, Tom Price affirmed the joy that emerges out of pain:

> Life goes on and you bear the unbearable and you endure the unendurable in faith that God is suffering with you. Faith in the God who cares is that "long red line" that runs through our lives and gives them meaning and joy.[19]

That "long red line" may be as close as we can get to what it meant for Mary to live with Simeon's warning. But by the alchemy of God's grace, our broken hearts can become the place where Christ is born again.

I leave the final word to Episcopal priest and author Lauren Winner who opened my eyes to Isaiah's very visceral metaphor of God as a woman in labor (Isa 42:14). She compared the vulnerability and pain of labor to God's broken heart at the cross:

> Perhaps God as a woman in travail can remind me of God's vulnerability, and the centrality of that vulnerability

18. Young, *United Methodist Hymnal*, 422.
19. Personal correspondence.

for my relationship with God. . . . Those moments when I stop fighting my own vulnerability are exactly the moments when I most participate in God's very nature, in God's life.[20]

I suspect Mary would agree!

---

20. Winner, *Wearing God*, 153–54.

4

Beginning at the End

"Jesus' mother . . . stood near the cross." (John 19:25)

I was one of the eighty-seven seniors in the graduating class of Clarion Area High School in 1965. We took our senior class trip from our county seat town in the hills of western Pennsylvania to New York City for the World's Fair. The dazzling collection of pavilions from corporations and nations from around the world was beyond our expectations. But nearly six decades later, I continue to be surprised by the exhibit I remember most clearly.

I didn't expect to appreciate the Vatican pavilion. Growing up in a rock-ribbed Protestant family in an equally Protestant-dominated town, I didn't know what the Catholics were doing inside the Church of the Immaculate Conception with its statues, candles, and crucifix, but I was pretty sure they were wrong. I reluctantly followed the tour guide into the pavilion to see the *Pietà*, Michelangelo's powerfully lifelike sculpture of Mary holding the lifeless body of Jesus in her arms. The tour book called it "The Crown Jewel of the Fair."

A surprising silence enveloped a crowd of noisy teenagers as we stepped onto the slowly moving walkways that carried us into the dark blue exhibit area where we viewed the statue through bullet-proof, ceiling-to-floor plexiglass panels. The visual impact

Beginning at the End

was as powerful as it was beautiful. I've never forgotten the way the light reflected from the perfectly white, smoothly carved marble; Mary's face looking down on Jesus' bruised body; the open gesture of her left hand inviting us to see and feel her immeasurable loss; the weight of Jesus' body resting limply in her lap, his right hand falling toward the ground.

Seven years later, Laszlo Toth surprised the world when he entered St. Peter's Basilica during the Pentecost service and attacked the *Pietà* with a geologist's hammer while shouting, "I am Jesus Christ! I have risen from the dead!" He hit Mary's figure fifteen times before bystanders wrestled him to the ground. The attack broke Mary's left arm at the elbow, knocked off part of her nose, and damaged one of her eyelids. The court judged Toth to be insane. He spent two years in an Italian psychiatric hospital, after which the authorities deported him to his native Australia. The sculpture was successfully repaired, but I felt as if a sword had pierced my heart.

A soul friend and pastoral colleague was in the eighth grade when he saw the *Pietà*. He names the visual impact of Mary holding the broken body of Jesus in her arms as a significant part of his journey toward embracing the meaning of the incarnation. He also remembers the pain that pierced his soul when he saw pictures of Toth's attack. The broken *Pietà* broke his heart. It became a significant step toward his call to ministry and planted the seeds of deep compassion in his life.

I share my memory of the *Pietà* to place the visual image of Mary cradling the lifeless body of her son in our imaginations as we step into the darkest hours in her story.

> *"When they arrived at the place called The Skull, they crucified him." (Luke 23:33)*

No one believed it would end this way! Jesus predicted it at least three times, but the power of denial is stubborn. Jesus' followers refused to accept the possibility that Jesus would die as a common criminal on a Roman cross. Simeon's grim warning haunted the dark corners of Mary's memory, but how could any mother believe that her son would end up naked, beaten, bleeding, and dying like this?

Our only contemporary comparison to the pain, humiliation, and sheer horror Mary experienced at Golgotha is the suffering of every heartbroken mother who stood by helplessly as her child became one of the 4,400 Black people who were lynched in the United States between 1877 and 1950. Their names are engraved on 800 blocks of Corten steel that hang above the heads of visitors to The National Memorial for Peace and Justice in Montgomery, Alabama, one for each county where a lynching took place. Friends from Tampa carried a jar of soil from the site where Tampa resident Robert Johnson was lynched on January 30, 1934, to the memorial. The jars memorialize the locations where the blood of lynching victims soaked the earth the way Jesus' blood soaked the earth beneath the cross.

African American theologian James H. Cone warned, "Until we can see the cross and the lynching tree together . . . there can be no genuine understanding of Christian identity in America, and no deliverance from the brutal legacy of slavery and white supremacy."[1]

Like death by lynching, death by crucifixion came slowly. Each gospel tells the story in its own way with its own purpose, but Matthew, Mark, and Luke agree Jesus hung there for about six hours. Drop by drop, Jesus' blood dripped from his torn flesh and soaked the ground. Every nerve ending was on fire. Every muscle not torn apart by the beating cramped in agony. Every desperate breath became an almost impossible accomplishment. Somewhere along the way, Jesus opened his eyes. Through tears and blood, "Jesus saw his mother" (John 19:26). And Mary saw Jesus seeing her. Pause with those words and try to touch the edge of what it meant to them to see each other at that moment. For Mary, it must have contained a lifetime of memories stretching all the way back to the day she said "yes" to the impossible possibility that she would give birth to the Son of God. It reminded Jesus of his responsibility as

---

1. Cone, *Cross and the Lynching Tree*, xv.

her first-born son. His last act of love was to entrust her into the care of his beloved disciple, John.

The gospels don't mention Mary by name again. Perhaps she went home with John right away. But how could she leave while her son was still alive? As a pastor, I've never seen a mother leave the hospital while her child was still breathing. Mary must have been among the women who stuck it out to the gruesome end. Perhaps she watched Nicodemus and Joseph of Arimathea yank Jesus' blood-soaked body free from nails. She may have helped anoint the body with the myrrh and aloe Nicodemus provided. She might have wrapped his body in a death shroud and helped lay him in the tomb the way she wrapped him in swaddling clothes and laid him in a manger. It's not in the gospels, but this is the poignant moment Michelangelo imagined when he carved the *Pietà*. I wonder if he wept while he carved it.

If Jesus' crucifixion doesn't send a shiver down our spines, we've become far too familiar with it. If the story no longer surprises us, we can understand why Lauren Winner confessed, "The Crucifixion has become so sanitized in my mind, so normalized and familiar, that thinking of it does not shock me . . . because I, along with much of the church, have turned a bloody state punishment into nothing more or less than tidy doctrine."[2]

How can the crucifixion be more than a "tidy doctrine" or a single event in the distant past? How can Mary's presence at the cross become a transformative metaphor for our life of faith? What on earth was Paul talking about when he declared, "We always carry Jesus' death around in our bodies so that Jesus' life can also be seen in our bodies" (2 Cor 4:10)?

"My God! My God, why?" (Mark 15:34)

If Mary stayed by the cross until the gruesome end, she heard Jesus shout the words of two prayers from the Psalms, prayers he

---

2. Winner, *Wearing God*, 154.

learned as a child at home or in synagogue in Nazareth. First, he remembered the opening lines of Psalm 22.

> My God! My God,
> > why have you left me all alone?
> > Why are you so far from saving me—
> > > so far from my anguished groans?
> >
> My God, I cry out during the day,
> > but you don't answer;
> > even at nighttime I don't stop. (Ps 22:1–2)

Put yourself in Mary's position. Imagine how it felt for a mother to hear her son scream, "My God! Why have you forsaken me?" (Matt 27:46; Mark 15:34, NRSV).

Matthew Shepherd's mother can probably hear her son cry those words in some deep corner of her broken heart. Twenty-two-year-old Matthew heard Jesus' cry of dereliction in his Episcopal Church on Good Friday. The words must have been in his heart and on his lips on the night of October 6, 1998, when two men beat him, tied him to a barbed-wire fence, and left him to die near Laramie, Wyoming, simply because he was gay. Reports said his face was covered in blood, except for places where tears ran down his cheeks.

"My God, why?" In Jesus' cry of utter abandonment, he identified with every God-forsaken moment of our God-loved lives in every God-forsaken corner of this God-loved world. We cannot go through any suffering, confront any evil, or sink to any depth of despair Jesus does not share with us. This is why Black slaves sang, "Nobody knows the trouble I've seen; Nobody knows but Jesus."

But there's more to Psalm 22 than the cry of dereliction. It also includes the transformative metaphor of God as a midwife.

> But you are the one who pulled me from the womb,
> > placing me safely at my mother's breasts.
> I was thrown on you from birth;
> > you've been my God
> > since I was in my mother's womb. (Ps 22:9–10)

You'll find the midwife metaphor again in Psalm 71:5–6:

> You, Lord, are the one I've trusted since childhood.
> I've depended on you from birth —
>> you cut the cord when I came from my mother's womb.

The midwife metaphor reminded Lauren Winner of Shifra and Puah, the Hebrew midwives who defied Pharoah's order to kill the baby boys in Egypt. It was similar to Herod's order to slaughter the boys in Bethlehem (Exod 1:19–20). Their act of civil disobedience became part of God's deliverance of the Hebrew people from slavery. The midwife metaphor also takes us back to Rachel's unnamed midwife who delivered Benjamin and was with Rachel when she died (Gen 35:16–18). Dr. Winner concluded, "The midwifing God is a God who helps bring about and sustain life. . . . The God who midwifes us is the God who delivers us."[3]

The Psalmist's soul-shattered cry also expresses deep trust in the God who gave us birth, who is with us in even in our darkest hour, and who will be with us in our death. One creed affirms:

> In life, in death, in life beyond death,
> God is with us.
> We are not alone.
> Thanks be to God.[4]

"After he said this, he breathed for the last time." (Luke 23:46)

The end came. Jesus' life ended in blood, sweat, and pain, not unlike the way it began when Mary gave birth to him. Jesus was born the way we are born. He died the way we die. On Ash Wednesday, the pastor places a dark stain on our foreheads with the unsettling words, "Remember that you are dust, and to dust you will return."

Kate Bowler was a thirty-five-year-old professor with a newly minted PhD and a promising career at Duke Divinity School. She was also a wife and the mother of a toddler son. The diagnosis of stage four cancer was a brutally intrusive surprise. The

---

3. Winner, *Wearing God*, 162–63.
4. Young, *United Methodist Hymnal*, 883.

only medical alternative was a trial program in immunotherapy. She was preparing for surgery to insert the port to pump chemotherapy drugs into her body when a physician's assistant surprised her by saying, "The sooner you get used to the idea of dying the better."[5] Early in the process she learned, "Start from the end and work backward."[6]

Starting from the end begins when we get used to the idea of dying. But who wants to do that? We are born to live! Sometimes death marks the termination of incomprehensible suffering as it did for Jesus. Sometimes it is the peaceful conclusion of a long and faithful life or the ultimate release from a mind that has lost all sense of its own identity. Sometimes it comes as the ruthless injustice of young lives that end in the fire of an assault weapon. But regardless of how it comes, death is always "the last enemy" (1 Cor 15:26). It is the uncompromising end of a story we hoped would go on, a performance we wish had one more act, or a game in which we wanted to play another quarter. That's why we whose parents have died find ourselves saying, "I wish they were here for this."

My father was only fifty-nine years old when he accepted the fact that he was dying. He chose to terminate the cancer treatments and made his arrangements with the funeral director, a long-time friend who lived across the street. He believed the promise of the resurrection. But he also spoke the truth during our last visit when he said, "I guess that's just how it is. There is always something we'd like to live just a little longer to see."

Accepting the reality of our death doesn't mean we have to like it. I hate death! I hate the way it tears away what might have been the continuation of our story. I resent the way death results from our insane addiction to violence. I detest the way the same evil powers of self-serving political partisanship, self-righteous bigotry, and relentless injustice that nailed Jesus to a cross continue to disrupt our lives and destroy God's creation. But we'd better get used to the fact that none of us will get out of here alive. A pastor and friend in South Africa said our problem is not that we die. We

5. Bowler, *No Cure*, 47.
6. Bowler, *No Cure*, 45.

can't do anything about that. Our problem is the fear and denial of death that prevent us from living the abundant life that Jesus came to bring before we die.

Here's the surprise. When we face up to the unwelcome reality of death, we discover how precious this life is and we can choose how we will live it. St. Benedict's "Rule" for his monasteries in the fifth century included the instruction, "Keep your death daily before your eyes." Reflecting on Benedict's dictum, Parker Palmer wrote, "That may sound like a morbid practice, but I assure you it isn't. If you hold a healthy awareness of your own mortality, your eyes will be opened to the glory and grandeur of life."[7] He said getting used to the idea of dying can evoke virtues of "hope, generosity, and gratitude."

"Blessed are those who mourn . . . " (Matt 5:4, KJV)

We face death with mourning. We flood our grief with our tears. I cannot count the number of times I began a funeral sermon with Shakespeare's final lines of *King Lear*, his most grief-soaked play.

> The weight of this sad time we must obey,
> Speak what we feel, not what we ought to say.[8]

When death comes, we easily slip into polite pastoral pablum or simplistic cultural chatter about death because we inherently resist its reality. We avoid the word with euphemisms like, "She's gone to sing with the angels," or "He went to that beautiful golf course in the sky." We tell ourselves, "Buck up! There's no need to cry." But we need to mourn and there's more than enough biblical precedent for crying.

- Jacob mourned beside Rachel's grave.
- The pages of the Psalms and the Prophets are soaked in tears.

---

7. Palmer, *On the Brink*, 49.
8. Shakespeare, *King Lear*, act 5, scene 3, line 392.

- The Hebrew people wept when they were refugees in Babylon and remembered the songs they sang in the Temple.
- The mothers of Bethlehem cried over the slaughter of their children.
- Jesus wept at the tomb of his friend Lazarus.
- He wept again as he looked out over Jerusalem and said, "If only you knew on this of all days the things that lead to peace" (Luke 19:41–42).
- Mary Magdalene was weeping in the garden when the risen Christ appeared to her.
- Paul did not say Christians don't mourn. He said we do not mourn "like others who don't have any hope" (1 Thess 4:13).
- Jesus promised, "Blessed are they that mourn: for they shall be comforted" (Matt 5:4, KJV).

But what's so "blessed" about mourning?

Nicholas Wolterstorff was a professor at Yale when his 25-year-old son, Eric, died in a mountain-climbing accident. He said he expects that for the rest of his life, he will see the world through his tears. That has certainly been the case for the parents I've known whose children died. But Wolterstorff also expressed his hope, "Perhaps I shall see things that dry-eyed I could not see."[9] Here are his words about Jesus' beatitude.

> The mourners are those who have glimpsed God's new day, who ache with all their being for the day's coming, and who break out into tears when confronted with its absence.... The mourners are aching visionaries.[10]

Wolterstoff's words inspired my reflections on this beatitude.

- Blessed are the "aching visionaries" who weep for the world the way it is because they can see how God intends for it to

---

9. Wolterstorff, *Lament for a Son*, 26.
10. Wolterstorff, *Lament for a Son*, 85.

be. They see the way it *will* be when God's kingdom fully comes, and God's will is fully done on earth.

- Blessed are those who mourn with confidence that one day, "the kingdoms of this earth will become the kingdoms of our God and of his Christ and he shall reign forever and ever" (Rev 11:15).

- Blessed are those who confront their loss, grief, and pain with the assurance, "Those who sow in tears will reap with shouts of joy" (Ps 126:5-6).

- Blessed are those who weep, knowing that one day God "will wipe every tear from their eyes. Death will be no more; mourning and crying and pain will be no more. For God will make all things new" (Rev 21:4).

- Blessed are faithful saints who mourn with the strong comfort of the presence of the One who died and rose again.

- Blessed are those who declare with Job, "I know that my Redeemer lives, and that at the last he will stand upon the earth" (Job 19:25, NRSV).

Here's the question: how does our dying shape our living? How can we "carry Jesus' death around in our bodies so that Jesus' life can also be seen in our bodies?" (2 Cor 4:10).

"I have been crucified with Christ . . . " (Gal 2:20)

Paul's crucifixion metaphor must have surprised the Galatians the first time they read his letter. They knew about Roman crucifixion. Some had seen it. They knew we can no more go back and be crucified with Christ than Nicodemus could go back into his mother's womb to be born again. Nor would they want to! What on earth was Paul talking about? Eugene Peterson's paraphrase helps bring Paul's words into our experience.

> I identified myself completely with him. Indeed, I have been crucified with Christ. My ego is no longer central. It

is no longer important that I appear righteous before you or have your good opinion, and I am no longer driven to impress God. Christ lives in me. The life you see me living is not "mine," but it is lived by faith in the Son of God, who loved me and gave himself for me. (Gal 2:20, MSG)

I once thought "being crucified with Christ" happened in an overpowering experience of spiritual surrender that would instantly change everything about what I thought, how I felt, and the way I lived. I grew up on the "holiness" branch of the Methodist family tree with its roots in the "camp meeting" movement in nineteenth-century America. I heard sermons about "entire sanctification" as a "second work of grace" in which the "sin nature" would be "eradicated" by the Holy Spirit. The sermons concluded with an "altar call" that indicated I could get it and get it now! As a college student I searched for that kind of dramatic spiritual encounter. But it never quite worked. No matter how sincerely I responded, I ended up dealing with the same old temptations, attitudes, and frustrations. I was not even aware at the time of my sinful infection of racism and white supremacy.

I'm grateful for the good gifts of the holiness tradition in my life. Those preachers planted within me a desire for a deeper life of faith. They got it right that if I want to become more like Christ there are things within me that need to be named, confessed, and surrendered at the cross. What they missed (or what I failed to hear!) was that John Wesley understood "Christian perfection" as a life that is continuously being shaped into the likeness of the love of God made flesh in Jesus and is expressed in social action. Historian and college colleague Irv A. Brendlinger said the holiness movement saw sanctification as "state" or "possession" rather than "relationship." They proclaimed it as something that happens in a moment rather than an ongoing work of God's Spirit that will only be completed in heaven. He showed how Wesley taught sanctification as "the empowering for a life of service, rather than a single religious experience that one would always be looking back to as an idol."[11]

11. Brendlinger, *Social Justice*, 111–12.

Beginning at the End

I now know being "crucified with Christ" is the ongoing pattern of the Christian life. Sanctification becomes a reality in ordinary, even tedious moments when I choose or am forced to surrender something I know about myself to all that I know about Christ. It's the way Jesus is born again and again through me. In daily surrender to Christ, Thomas Merton found "the innocence and liberty of soul that come to those who have thrown away all preoccupation with themselves and their own ideas and judgement and opinions and desires, and are perfectly content to take things as they come to them from the hand of God."[12]

Here's how practical the process of sanctification can become. I was deeply engaged in one of those all-too-common but frustratingly intractable times of tension in the church. Living into my identity as a first-born child, I thought I alone could fix it. I was driven by my need to be at the center of everything and was working hard to impress everyone around me. In my over-confidence, I was pretty sure that I got it right and everyone else was mistaken. But it wasn't working. My frustration ate away at my soul, robbed me of joy, and infected my relationships with other people. Finally, a wise friend looked me squarely in the eye and said, "Jim, this is *so* not about you!" It was the gift I needed then and have needed again and again. It was an invitation to self-differentiation in a conflicted situation so I could be part of the solution rather than being part of the problem. I was challenged not to think of myself more highly than I ought to think (Rom 12:3).

Sometimes it *is* about me. Sometimes it is about my ego, my need for approval, my desire to impress or please everyone, or the anxiety I pour into the situation. In those times I am called to acknowledge my limitations, confess my arrogant attitudes, and seek forgiveness from God and people I hurt along the way. It's part of the process of being crucified with Christ, so that his life can be formed in me. It's the cruciform way of life Paul copied from a hymn or affirmation of the early church.

Adopt the attitude that was in Christ Jesus.

---

12. Merton, *Seven Storey Mountain*, 388.

> Though he was in the form of God,
>> he did not consider being equal with God something to exploit.
> But he emptied himself
>> by taking the form of a slave
>> and by becoming like human beings.
> When he found himself in the form of a human,
>> he humbled himself by becoming obedient to the point of death,
>>> even death on a cross. (Phil 2:6–8)

Karen Armstrong, British author and scholar in comparative religion, pointed us in this direction when she wrote, "One way or another, we have to leave behind our inbuilt selfishness, with its greedy fears and cravings.... We are most creative and sense other possibilities that transcend our ordinary experience when we leave ourselves behind."[13] In leaving ourselves behind, we are set free to follow Christ. In dying to ourselves, we allow space for the risen Christ to become alive in us again.

> *"They rested on the Sabbath, in keeping with the commandment." (Luke 23:56)*

The Good Friday Tenebrae service ends. The gospel stories have been read. The last candle is extinguished. The altar is stripped. The Christ candle is carried from the darkened sanctuary. There's a breathless moment in darkness before the lights come up. We walk out in somber silence. Darkness has fallen on the earth. Holy Saturday comes. And we wait.

I was working on this chapter when "breaking news" popped up on my screen. Another uniquely American assault rifle attack on a Nashville school resulted in the deaths of three children, three adults on the staff, and the shooter. Shortly after the news broke, I received a shocking email from a ministerial colleague.

> Hey . . . I'm numb. . . . The shooter was the child of my dear neighbors. . . . A mass of unmarked police vehicles

---

13. Armstrong, *Spiral Staircase*, 278–79.

with blue lights descended on my street. SWAT officers stormed the house, using a grenade to blow off the front door. I watched it all from my living room window before a police officer yelled at me to "get down." I'm numb ... completely, utterly numb.... Crime scene tape is wrapped around my mailbox to the end of the street.... I'm just numb ...

The words left me numb as well. I sat in silence, stunned beyond words, not at all sure how to respond. The news reports of the shooting were bad enough, but I never expected to be drawn into the tragedy through another person's experience. I tried to picture the neighbor's house with its door blown open. I wondered what would be next. What would happen to the neighbor? How would my friend heal from the shock? Where would the story go from here?

Numb. That word must have described the women who came with Jesus from Galilee. They stood with Mary near the cross. They watched Jesus take his last breath. They saw his body laid in the tomb. They went to wherever they were staying in the city, frozen by the shock, speechless with grief too deep to express, aching with pain too overpowering to avoid. I'm sure they tried, as we all try, to make death manageable by repeating the story again and again. Someone remembered Jesus' last words, "Father, into your hands I entrust my life" (Luke 23:46). They knew Jesus was quoting Psalm 31. When I live with that psalm, I experience the psalmist rocking back and forth on waves of conflicting emotions, from faith to fear and from despair to hope. The writer prays in desperation.

> Please never let me be put to shame.
>   Rescue me by your righteousness!
> Deliver me quickly;
>   be a rock that protects me;
>   be a strong fortress that saves me!

> Have mercy on me, Lord, because I'm depressed.
>   My vision fails because of my grief....
> My life is consumed with sadness;
>   my years are consumed with groaning.

> I am forgotten, like I'm dead,
> > completely out of mind;
> > I am like a piece of pottery, destroyed.

You can't get much lower than that! But in the depths of desperation, the psalmist clings to the assurance of God's unchanging faithfulness and steadfast love.

> I entrust my spirit into your hands;
> > you, Lord, God of faithfulness—
> > you have saved me. . . .
> I rejoice and celebrate in your faithful love
> > because you saw my suffering—
> > you were intimately acquainted with my deep distress.
> You didn't hand me over to the enemy,
> > but set my feet in wide-open spaces. . . .
> I trust you, Lord!
> > I affirm, "You are my God."
> My future is in your hands. . . .

The psalm ends with a challenge for all of us.

> All you who are faithful, love the Lord! . . .
> All you who wait for the Lord,
> > be strong and let your heart take courage.

The gospel says Mary went home with John. Wherever she was, I'm sure her friends were with her. I've seen the way faithful women stick together!

I imagine Mary's friends were like the powerful women in the movie *Steel Magnolias*. They stayed at the cemetery with M'Lynn after the burial of her daughter, Shelby, who died giving birth to a son. When the ever-naïve Annelle offered comfort with sentiments of simplistic piety, M'Lynn said her mind told her she needed to move on, but she wished someone would tell that to her heart. She described the way the men in the family left her alone at the hospital. She named the awesome and awful privilege of being there when her daughter was born and being there when she died. With that, she lost control of her emotions. She stormed away from the grave as she shouted the question every sorrowing mother asks, "God, why?"

Mary must have had an explosion of grief like that in the aftermath of her son's burial. Let's not make her out to be more pious than the psalmist or more faithful than Jesus. The psalmists never hesitate to name their deepest fear, guilt, anger, and grief. Jesus prayed with gut-wrenching honesty in Gethsemane when he pleaded with God to find some other way to fulfill his mission. But in their darkest hour, both Jesus and the psalmists trusted their life and their death into the steadfast love and unyielding faithfulness of God. And they waited.

We will not be fully prepared for the surprise on Sunday morning until we wait in stunned sorrow with the women in Saturday's stony silence. In the traditional service for Holy Saturday, we pray, "Grant that we may *await with him* the dawning of the third day and rise to newness of life."[14] Don't miss that we wait "*with him.*" Jesus is with us in the tomb. He waits with us in the numbness of death for the resurrection to new life. We wait in hope.

"I wait for God's promise." (Ps 130:5)

I began this chapter with Michelangelo's incomparable *Pietà*. I discovered a contemporary wood carving of the theme at Durham Cathedral in England. It stands in an open space where I could reach out to touch it.

Fenwick Lawson completed his interpretation of the *Pietà* in 1981 after seven years of work. The life-size figure of Mary stands beside the broken body of Jesus, which is stretched out on the floor. His right arm lies broken beside his body. The natural cracks in the tree from which Mary was carved became a visual expression of her tears. Lawson's figures were on display in York Minster in 1984 when the roof caught fire directly above the carving. Molten lead dropped like tears on Mary's brow. The heat caused cracks in her

---

14. Neil, *Book of Worship*, 366, italics added.

face to split wider. Falling debris singed the Christ figure and splattered it with lead. But far from destroying the figures, the damage increased their emotional impact.

The unnerving surprise is that Mary reaches down toward Jesus with her right hand and Jesus' left arm stretches up toward her. I assumed the artist intended it to express the stiffness of rigor mortis. Another interpretation is that Lawson intended it as Jesus reaching up to the one who gave him life as a sign of the hope of resurrection. In the hour of suffering, defeat, despair, or death, we reach out in hope that we will be raised to new life. We wait with the psalmist:

> I hope, Lord.
> My whole being hopes,
>   and I wait for God's promise.
> My whole being waits for my Lord—
>   more than the night watch waits for morning;
>   yes, more than the night watch waits for morning!
>
> Israel, wait for the Lord!
>   Because faithful love is with the Lord;
>   because great redemption is with our God! (Ps 130:5–7)

Jurgen Moltmann was a seventeen-year-old student from a secular family who intended to study mathematics and physics. He remembers the night in 1943 when the bombs fell on his hometown of Hamburg, Germany, destroying the city and killing 40,000 residents. In the darkness of that catastrophic night, he cried out for the first time, "God, where are you?" He struggled with that question during three years as a prisoner of war in Scotland during which a chaplain gave him a Bible. He was surprised by the way he identified with the psalms of lament. When he read Mark's gospel and heard Jesus ask, "My God, why have you forsaken me?," Moltmann said, "I felt he understood me. That gave me new courage to live.... That was my new beginning, the beginning I arrived at when Hamburg was at its end; in the end was my beginning."[15]

---

15. Moltmann, *In the End*, 34–35.

Beginning at the End

After the war, he became one of the leading theologians of our time. He wrote, "If Christ's farewell in his death has become the new, eternal beginning of his resurrection, then in our end we too shall find our new, eternal beginning.... So, death is the end, but not the last of all. Something else will come."[16]

I close this chapter with words that speak to both the end and the hope of a new beginning. They were written by Samuel Wesley, the father of John and Charles, and were among his records that were found in the ashes of the Epworth rectory fire in 1709.

> Behold the Savior of mankind
> Nailed to the shameful tree!
> How vast the love that Him inclined
> To bleed and die for thee!
>
> 'Tis done! the precious ransom's paid!
> "Receive my soul!" He cries;
> See where He bows His sacred head!
> He bows His head and dies!
>
> But soon He'll break death's envious chain,
> And in full glory shine;
> O Lamb of God, was ever pain,
> Was ever love, like Thine?[17]

---

16. Moltmann, *In the End*, 100.
17. Young, *United Methodist Hymnal*, 293.

5

Bending the Time

"In the depths of who I am, I rejoice in God my savior." (Luke 1:46)

Where was Mary when she heard the news? Who told Jesus' mother about the empty tomb?

Mary's name doesn't appear in the resurrection stories. If she was, as tradition tells us, a primary source for Luke's gospel, why didn't he include her version of the Easter story in his gospel? Historians, theologians, Popes, and Sunday School teachers have tried to answer the question of Mary's absence from the text. Speaking as a mother and grandmother, my wife is sure Jesus' mother was there! Where else would a mother be? I see the empty space in the gospel as an invitation to imagine where she was and what she was doing as the sun rose that Sunday morning.

I picture Mary with the remnant of Jesus' followers behind a locked door in a quiet corner of Jerusalem. They were hiding in fear, expecting the same authorities who crucified their master to come for his followers as well. They were, after all, at the center of the political protest that paraded Jesus into the city on Sunday. Jesus' closest companions were with him in Gethsemane when the guards arrested him. They lingered at the edge of the crowd at Golgotha, watching in horror the way Rome dealt with anyone who fomented an insurrection against the Empire. The men ran away, but the women stayed to the gruesome end. They followed his body to the tomb. Wherever they were hiding on that somber Saturday, they were engulfed in mind-numbing despair and soul-draining grief.

Suddenly, just as the sun was rising, the women who went to embalm the body came rushing through the door. Gasping for air, with sweat from the early morning heat dripping down their foreheads, they chattered over each other through breathless shock and unrelenting tears, "We went to take care of the body, just the way we had planned." Their voices quivered, "But when we got there. . . ." Their bodies shaking, they went on, "The stone they rolled in front of the tomb and stamped with Pilate's seal was pushed aside, knocked over, rolled away!" Stupefied by the surprise, Mary Magdalene stammered, "Some strange men were standing by the entrance. We froze, too afraid to move." Halting, not sure she dared to believe what she was saying, she blurted out the news, "They said we were looking in the wrong place, though God knows there was no mistaking where we laid his body!" The words were flowing quickly now. She declared the unbelievable announcement, "The men told us he had been raised and was on the road ahead of us! They said he was going to Galilee and would meet us there!"

Silence! Everyone in the room was speechless, stunned, and still. Peter ran to check it out, but John outran him and got to the tomb first. Mary Magdalene sneaked away to return to the garden alone. Everyone in the room turned to Jesus' mother to see how she would respond. It was the way we watch the surviving spouse or the parent of the deceased child to take our cue from them. As they watched and waited, I hope they caught the faintest hint of a subtle, knowing smile through Mary's grief. Sometime during those long, pain-soaked hours, they might have even heard something close to laughter; not giddy or silly laughter, but a surprising warmth that percolated from a soul drained of tears. It arose from the crack in her broken heart resulting from the sword Simeon predicted would pierce her inner being. In the depths of her grief, she knew something no one else thought could happen had happened!

As she began to recover from the shock of what she had seen and heard, I hope Mary found moments in which she laughed with the kind of laughter that takes us by surprise at the sheer audacity of a seemingly impossible promise coming true. I hope she laughed the way Jesus described the joy of a woman whose baby arrives after painful labor and the way Sarah and Abraham laughed when the angel said they would give birth and would end up with as many children as the stars in the sky. I hope she laughed like the woman in Proverbs who "laughs at the time to come" (Prov 31:25, NRSV). I hope Mary wept with what Frederick Buechner described as "glad tears at last . . . tears at the hilarious unexpectedness of things rather than at their tragic expectedness."[1] I hope the rest of Jesus' followers heard in her laughter the laughter of God. Lauren Winner underscores God's laughter in Psalm 2 and Psalm 37 where "God is laughing because God knows that ultimately the unjust will not triumph."[2]

If Mary laughed, and I'm pretty sure she did, it was a deeper, pain-soaked version of the laughter with which people responded to the unexpected surprise in the stories Jesus told about the Samaritan they all hated who turned out to be the hero; the repentant sinner who went home rejoicing instead of the self-righteous pharisee; or the extravagant father who threw a welcome home party for his runaway son while the elder brother sulked on the front porch and refused to come in. It's the smile on our face when a story suddenly turns in a direction we never expected but which turns out to be the only ending that can satisfy our deepest hunger and highest hopes. It's the joy that takes our breath away when the beast we thought was dead turns into a prince; Sleeping Beauty is awakened with a kiss; Aslan breaks the wintery curse over Narnia and spring comes again.

Our family shared that kind of unexpected laughter when we gathered around a lunch table following the memorial service for a long-time friend. We were still wearing our funeral clothes, trying to accept the fact that he was gone, remembering all we shared in the past, and thinking of the things we would miss in the future.

1. Buechner, *Telling the Truth*, 61.
2. Winner, *Wearing God*, 186.

Our daughter gently interrupted the conversation to say, "I think we need some good news." Everyone gave her their full attention. She said very simply, "I'm pregnant." There was a moment of stunned silence. It was unexpected news because she and her husband had completed many rounds of infertility treatments and had been unable to conceive. My mouth dropped wide open in speechless surprise. My wife shouted, "Deborah! That's wonderful!" Everyone around the table broke out in tear-filled laughter. The unexpected had happened! What appeared to be impossible became possible. We laughed at the joyful promise of new life even as we wept over the painful reality of death.

I don't know how Mary got the news. The stories of what happened that morning tumble over each other in the four gospels making it nearly impossible to compose a linear narrative. At first, the disciples thought it was the foolish chatter of women, but by the end of that first resurrection day, just about everyone started believing the unbelievable except for Thomas. He might have been the only person who was honest enough to declare what other folks were feeling but were afraid to say. A week later, after Jesus invited him to touch the print of the nails and the scar in his side, Thomas started believing it, too! They could not explain how it happened. They never tried. But they knew Jesus was alive! It was as if he had been born again among them.

Amid the excited confusion, I suspect Mary remembered the song she sang at the beginning of her story.

> With all my heart I glorify the Lord!
> In the depths of who I am I rejoice in God my savior....
> He has shown strength with his arm.
> He has scattered those with arrogant thoughts and proud inclinations.
> He has pulled the powerful down from their thrones
> and lifted up the lowly....
> He has come to the aid of his servant Israel,
> remembering his mercy,
> just as he promised to our ancestors,
> to Abraham and to Abraham's descendants forever.
>
> (Luke 1:47–55)

How can Mary's untold resurrection story become a transformative metaphor for the way the risen Christ comes alive in and through us?

> *"In fact, Christ has been raised from the dead."*
> *(1 Cor 15:20, NRSV)*

I picture Mary among the disciples in the "upper room" on Sunday evening when "Jesus came and stood among them" (John 20:19) despite the doors being closed in fear. I suspect she was the only person in the room who wasn't totally surprised. Somewhere deep in her heart, she must have believed the powers of evil, injustice, sin, and death could not defeat the son who was born through her body. For everyone else, the resurrection was an unmitigated surprise. They knew death was the end. No one expected a new beginning. No one really believed it would happen, at least not here, not in this place, not at this time, not even for the Son of God.

Faithful Jews who believed in resurrection were like Martha, Lazarus's sister. Standing beside her brother's tomb, she told Jesus through her tears, "I know that he will rise in the resurrection on the last day." It never occurred to her that resurrection might happen right here, right now. But Jesus replied, "I am the resurrection and the life. Whoever believes in me will live, even though they die. Everyone who lives and believes in me will never die. Do you believe this?" (John 11:25–26). Don't miss the present tense verbs *am, believes, lives*. On Easter morning, the church shouts the good news in the emphatic present tense, "Christ *is* risen! Christ *is* risen, indeed!" The risen Christ asks the same question Jesus asked Mary, "Do you believe this?"

Believing in the resurrection is more than remembering an inexplicable event in the past. I've never heard an attempt at a rational explanation of what happened inside the tomb that makes much sense. The chief priests peddled the only reasonable "alternative fact." They paid the guards to say Jesus' followers stole the body while they were sleeping (Matt 28:11–15). The priests clearly didn't know these disciples! The possibility that they could get away with a heist like that seems very unlikely!

The vacated tomb alone wasn't enough to convince Jesus' followers that he was alive and walking with them. They came to believe in the resurrection as they experienced Jesus standing among them in ordinary places in extraordinary ways.

- Mary Magdalene met Jesus in the garden but thought he was the gardener until he spoke her name.
- Cleopas and an unnamed follower walked with Christ to Emmaus, but didn't recognize him until he broke the bread at their dinner table.
- The disciples did not know it was Jesus until he showed them the scars on his hands and side.
- Peter and the six former fishermen were surprised when Jesus had breakfast waiting for them on the beach after their botched attempt to return to their old profession. During breakfast, Jesus renewed Peter's calling despite his catastrophic denial.

Luke says Jesus' appearances kept happening. For forty days, "He showed them that he was alive with many convincing proofs" (Acts 1:3). We get the impression that the risen Christ can show up just about anytime, anywhere. The resurrection becomes a self-proving reality as his disciples live into it. The stories led E. Stanley Jones to pray, "O You hidden, universal Christ, I cannot turn anywhere without confronting You. For I meet You on every road, the road of the Scriptures and the road of life."[3]

Jerusha Matsen Neal experienced the presence of the risen Christ during morning worship in the chapel of the Davuilevu Training College, the oldest seminary in the Fiji Islands. The service began in silence. When the choir leader gave the pitch, the congregation began singing in their native iTaukei language,

---

3. Jones, *Way*, 180.

"Jesus, stand among us, in your risen power." Dr. Neal wrote, "On this particular morning, I believe he does."[4]

But there's more!

> *"We always carry Jesus' death around in our bodies so that Jesus' life can also be seen in our bodies." (1 Cor 4:10)*

Paul never met Mary, but he met her son on the road to Damascus. In his mind-boggling assertion to the Corinthians, he claimed the extraordinary, once-for-all-time death and resurrection of Jesus can become a present-day, flesh-and-blood reality in our ordinary human bodies. How can we become men and women through whom the life and death of Jesus are alive in our world today?

A living metaphor of Paul's astounding affirmation took me by surprise when I stumbled into a YouTube recording of the internationally acclaimed conductor John Eliot Gardiner conducting the Monteverdi Choir and the Paris Philharmonic Orchestra in a performance of Johann Sebastian Bach's *Mass in B Minor*. I realize a Bach mass is not everyone's preferred style of worship music but stick with me for the sake of the metaphor!

Gardiner grew up singing Bach chorales in his home and in the local church choir. An original portrait of Bach hung on the wall of their home. A German friend sent the painting to the Gardiners for safekeeping in England during World War II. Gardiner began conducting at fifteen. Across years, he became an authority on Bach by studying, practicing, hearing, and playing Bach's music.

The chorus stood and the audience applauded as Gardiner stepped onto the stage. He humbly acknowledged the audience, smiled at the singers, and closed his eyes for an extended period of silence. Was he in prayer? Or was he opening some deep part of himself to Bach's presence in the music? He lifted his head slowly and began conducting the entire piece from memory without the score in front of him. He had taken the music so deeply into himself it permeated every movement of his body, every gesture of his

---

4. Neal, *Overshadowed Preacher*, 1.

hands, every expression on his face. It was as if Bach was born again through the conductor's body.

Gardiner paused at the end of the musically complex and emotionally powerful *Sanctus* to replenish his strength. He wiped sweat from his forehead and took a drink of water before charging full strength into the *Credo*. When the music ended there was a moment of utter stillness before everyone in the audience rose to their feet in thunderous applause. Again, Gardiner humbly acknowledged the applause and recognized the musicians. He smiled the way people smile when they know they have been a part of something greater than themselves.

If Bach is not your idea of a good time, I invite you to remember the way Gregory Peck channeled Atticus Finch in the movie classic *To Kill A Mockingbird*. Jeff Daniels and Richard Thomas recently portrayed Atticus on Broadway. In each case, the actors absorbed Harper Lee's character into themselves so that his words and actions came alive through their own unique voices and different bodies.

It's an imperfect metaphor, as all metaphors are, but it can be a human metaphor of a spiritual reality. We cannot literally become Jesus any more than Gardiner could literally become Bach, or the actors become Atticus Finch. We cannot literally carry Jesus' death and resurrection in our bodies any more than we can go back into our mother's womb to be born again. But we can absorb Jesus' words. We can watch the way he lived, center ourselves in the way he died, and experience the way he stands among us. We can keep our eyes open to see the evidence of his living presence in the lives of others. We can absorb the life of Jesus into our body the way Gardiner absorbed Bach's music so that just as something of the composer came alive through the body of the conductor, the living Christ can come alive in us. Bonhoeffer said we are "given the incomprehensibly great promise that . . . the image of Christ . . . enters, permeates, and transforms [us] so that [we] become like [our] master."[5] This was, in fact, the promise Jesus left with his disciples at the last supper when he told them the Comforter, the

---

5. Bonhoeffer, *Discipleship*, 281.

Spirit of Truth, would live within us, reminding us of everything he said (John 15:16–17).

Jesus' promise continues to be fulfilled. Through the power of the Holy Spirit, the death and resurrection of Jesus still becomes a flesh and blood reality among us. I've seen it happen through men and women like Jim Estep. I did not know Jim. I attended his memorial service because his daughter is a clergy colleague and friend. Listening to the stories people told about him and ways he impacted their lives, I felt as if Jim was standing among us. After he died, his family found a note in his Bible with words he labeled as his "Personal Creed." It read, "Live in such a way that those who know you but don't know Jesus, will come to know Jesus because they know you." The stories people told confirmed that it worked! People got to know the living Christ as they got to know Jim Estep.

But wait! There's more!

> *"So then, if anyone is in Christ, that person is part of the new creation. The old things have gone away, and look, new things have arrived!" (2 Cor 5:17)*

Believing in the resurrection, we become part of God's new creation, indeed, God's *re-creation*, of the world. Resurrection is not only an event in the past, a personal experience for individual disciples, or the grand finale of history when the whole broken creation will be made new. Jesus' resurrection bends time to bring what happened in the past into the present in a way that reshapes the way we live into the future.

You may have heard a preacher or teacher point out the two New Testament Greek words for "time." The word *chronos* names what we measure in minutes, hours, or days. The Broadway musical *Rent* counts *chronos* as "five hundred twenty-five thousand, six hundred minutes" in a year. It's what we mean when we ask, "What time is it?" or "When will the grandchildren arrive?" The lyrics in *Rent* go on to celebrate what the Greeks called *kairos*. It is time determined by the importance of what we experience in it. It's what we mean when we exclaim, "We had a wonderful time with the grandchildren!" The musical measures time "In truths that she learned / Or in times that he cried / In bridges he burned / Or the way that she died."[6]

Jesus' resurrection in chronological time becomes timelessly transformative in history and in everyone who, in Jesus' words, "lives and believes" in him. A colleague compared the resurrection to a door that opened to allow the future to come in and invites us to walk through it. In *Christianity's Surprise,* Kavin Rowe wrote:

> Jesus' resurrection showed the future, what God intended for humanity, and that future was now present, here, and creating a new world . . . [it] created a new sense of time. And that new sense of time created a new sense of how to be in the world. . . . God's good future for humanity had arrived in the present and beckoned us forward; the time was that of new creation in the midst of the old.[7]

Here's a cosmic metaphor. A long-awaited Christmas gift arrived on December 25, 2021, when the James Webb telescope began "a million-mile trip to the morning of time." Leaders of the project were as excited as children opening their gifts under the tree. Thomas Zurbuchen, NASA's associate administrator for science, said, "Every time we launch a big, bold telescope, we get a surprise." Astronomer Alan Dressler shouted, "Hallelujah!—a sacred word for the moment."[8]

In ways that are totally beyond my comprehension, the Webb telescope will enable scientists to see, in the present, the earliest galaxies that formed after the big bang and led to the formation of our solar system. The Webb telescope is, in fact, bending time to bring the incomprehensible past into the present in a way that points toward the future.

As fantastic as the metaphor might be, it is no more extravagant than the astonishing claim the first Christians affirmed in an early creed or hymn.

---

6. Larson, "Seasons of Love," para. 6.
7. Rowe, *Christianity's Surprise,* 20–21, 33.
8 Overbye, "James Webb Telescope Launches," paras. 8, 29.

> The Son is the image of the invisible God,
> > the one who is first over all creation,
> Because all things were created by him:
> > both in the heavens and on the earth,
> > the things that are visible and the things that are invisible . . .
>
> He existed before all things,
> > and all things are held together in him. . . .
>
> Because all the fullness of God was pleased to live in him,
> > and he reconciled all things to himself through him—
> > whether things on earth or in the heavens.
> > > He brought peace through the blood of his cross.
>
> (Col 1:15-20)

The affirmation is audacious! Brazen! Bold! Not restricted to prior assumptions or ideas. Extravagantly original, daringly courageous, and, sometimes, downright frightening! If we believe the son born through Mary is the visible, finite image of the invisible, infinite God, it means that in Jesus' life, death, and resurrection we see the essential character of the God through whom all creation came into being and in whom this damaged creation will ultimately be reconciled and made whole.

Believing in the resurrection means we dare to live as if the kingdom of God that Jesus defined in his words, demonstrated in his life, and promised God would fulfill in the future, is becoming a reality in the present in anticipation of its fulfillment when *chronos* time will be no more. God's "new creation" of a world of love, justice, and peace is already here! By the power of the Holy Spirit, we become participants in the answer to the prayer for God's kingdom to come and God's will to be done on earth, even as it is already done in heaven. Jesus stands among us as we live now in ways that are consistent with the way the world will one day be. We become a present, finite, imperfect expression of the infinite, perfect purpose of God made flesh in the death and resurrection of Jesus.

Bending the Time

"He is going ahead of you into Galilee. You will see him there."
(Mark 16:7)

Here's a fact that is as obvious as it is easily overlooked. None of the people in the resurrection narratives were fully aware of what was happening or of what it would mean in the future. Mary, Peter, John, Thomas, Mary Magdalene: none of them felt the earthquake shake the tomb. They didn't see the stone roll away from the entrance. They weren't present when Jesus walked out of the darkness of death into the light of the new day. They received the news of the resurrection in silence. There were no blaring trumpets, no massed choirs singing Handel's "Hallelujah," no churches filled with worshippers shouting, "He is risen, indeed!" No wonder Mark concluded the first account of that morning with the disconcerting words, "Overcome with terror and dread, they fled from the tomb. They said nothing to anyone because they were afraid" (Mark 16:8).

Even as they began to believe that Jesus was alive, they had no clue as to how the early church would come to understand the time-bending, history-shaping, life-transforming implications of what happened. It would take fifty days for them to be prepared for the infusive power of the Holy Spirit to blow like the wind and burn like fire within them on Pentecost. In Acts, the apostles are consistently surprised by what happens in, through, and around them. They never imagined how their experience of the risen Christ would energize a movement that would sweep across the Roman Empire and reshape human history. They had no idea of the challenges that were ahead of them. But they received the promise that the risen Christ was going before them and that, whatever the future might hold, they would find him there.

The good news we proclaim on Easter is not simply that Jesus rose in the past or that we will be with him in heaven when we die, but that Christ is here with us now. Christ goes before us into an unpredictable future, and we can trust him to meet us there. In the preface to his classic, *The Cost of Discipleship*, Dietrich Bonhoeffer wrote, "Only Jesus Christ, who bids us follow him, knows where the path will lead. But we know it will be a path full of mercy beyond measure. Discipleship is joy."[9]

A fellow pastor shared the story of a member of his congregation who was a prisoner of war in a Japanese internment camp during WWII. The conditions were horrendous; it was a miracle he survived. The former prisoner said that one of the things that kept him going was remembering the hymns he learned while growing up in the church. He specifically remembered "Christ the Lord Is Risen Today." The words assured him that Christ was with him even when "today" was the worst of days.

> *"The divine 'yes' has at last sounded in him."*
> *(2 Cor 1:19, MOFF)*

Mary's story began with her "yes" to Gabriel's invitation to be the woman through whom Christ would be born. Simeon confirmed her "yes" when he warned that a sword would pierce her innermost being. She heard Jesus' first "yes" in the temple when he was twelve years old. We saw it when he resisted temptation in the wilderness. We heard it again in Gethsemane when he prayed, "My Father, if it's not possible that this cup be taken away unless I drink it, then let it be what you want" (Matt 36:42). Their obedience led Jesus and Mary to the suffering of the cross and the darkness of Joseph's tomb. The powers of evil, injustice, and death declared their final "no!" in the funereal thud of the stone that blocked the entrance. But on the third day, God spoke the last word when "the divine yes" shattered the stony darkness of death.

Paul offered his "yes" in obedience to Christ's unexpected call on the Damascus Road. Like Mary, his "yes" took him to difficult and dangerous places. He was reflecting on one of those distressing times when he wrote:

> The Son of God, Jesus Christ, who was proclaimed among you by us (by myself and Silvanus and Timotheus) was not "yes and no"—the divine "yes" has at last

---

9. Bonhoeffer, *Discipleship*, 40.

sounded in him, for in him is the "yes" that affirms all the promises of God. Hence it is through him that we affirm our "amen" in worship, to the glory of God. (Acts 26:19, MOFF)

Because of the resurrection, we know the worst word is never the last word. God's word was, is, and always will be, "yes!" The resurrection confirmed the confidence with which Martin Luther King Jr. said there is a moral arc in the universe that bends toward justice. Jon Meacham pointed to Abraham Lincoln as an example of how "even the most imperfect of people . . . can help bend the arc."[10]

Easter morning worshippers at the two-hundred-year-old Union United Methodist Church in Boston's South End celebrated the way one person's "yes" is bending that arc toward justice. Justin Jamal Pearson was part of their congregation before he returned to Memphis and became the duly elected member of the Tennessee House of Representatives. The white members of the House expelled him on Thursday of Holy Week because he joined two other members in protesting the legislature's inaction on gun violence. Their action came in response to the deaths of three children and three adults at the Covenant School in Nashville.

Representative Pearson sent a word of hope to the congregation by video. "How is it that even now, with mass persecution on this Holy Week, that we still have a hope? It's because even from the bottom of slave ships, my people didn't quit. Even in cotton fields and rice fields. My people didn't quit."[11] One church member said of Pearson, "He's channeling MLK!"

Ministerial colleague Ted Crass described his experience with Justin Pearson in a small group at Union. Ted wrote, "I learned a lot from him. We live in the land of the free / home of the brave, but for many, church is the only place that folks experience true freedom. The resistance to the powers and the rooting of his hope

10. Meacham, *And There Was Light*, xx.
11. Martin, "One of the Exiled," para. 10.

and action in God's faithfulness has been inspiring. Keep your eye on him."[12]

Six days after his expulsion and three days into the "Great Fifty Days" of Easter, the Shelby County Board of Commissioners voted unanimously to reappoint Pearson to the Tennessee House. Through it all, he became a nationally recognized participant in bending the moral arc of our history toward justice and freedom. His "yes" bears witness to the divine "yes" in the hope of the resurrection.

"As in Adam all die, even so in Christ shall all be made alive."
(1 Cor 15:22, KJV)

It was sacred pastoral privilege to place my hand on the caskets of faithful people and pray over their open graves:

> Almighty God,
> into your hands we commend your *son / daughter [Name]*,
> in sure and certain hope of resurrection to eternal life
> through Jesus Christ our Lord. Amen.[13]

Jesus died. But death was not the end for Jesus, and it will not be the end for us. We live and we die with the assurance, "The one who raised Christ from the dead will give life to your human bodies also, through his Spirit that lives in you" (Rom 8:11).

The early Christians did not accept the Platonic idea of the "immortality of the soul." It assumed (and still assumes) there is an essential, disembodied part of us that dwells within this disposable shell and leaves the body behind to go on living after the body dies. Because of their experience of the resurrection, they proclaimed the far more radical understanding. In his foundational treatise in 1 Corinthians 15, Paul proclaimed the resurrection of the body as God's intrusive action that overcomes the power of death and raises us to new life in the resurrection.[14] The revolutionary promise

---

12. Personal correspondence.
13. Alexander, *Book of Worship*, 156.
14. A good starting point for more complete discussion of this subject is Wright, *Surprised by Hope*.

of Easter faith is that just as God raised Jesus to new life, God will raise us as well. This promise led Jurgen Moltmann to write:

> In faith in the Christ risen from the dead, the "perhaps" becomes a certainty.... If Christ's farewell in his death has become the new eternal beginning in his resurrection, then in our end we too shall find our new, eternal beginning.[15]

More than fifty years later, I still remember a fellow seminary student who was serving a rural congregation. One day his two young sons went with him to the cemetery for a burial. Before the casket and the family arrived, the boys were peering down into the open grave. The younger son asked, "Is that what happens when you die? They put you down into a big hole?" Before my friend could come up with an age-appropriate, biblically accurate, theologically sound answer, the older brother replied, "Yea! That's what happens. But don't worry, Jesus can get you out of that hole!" When my fellow student told the story, he simply concluded, "There was no way for me to improve on that answer." I've never improved on it, either!

I do not know why the gospel writers left Mary's name out of the resurrection narratives. I don't know where she was or what she was doing when she heard about the empty tomb. I intend to ask Luke why he left her out when I meet him in heaven! I don't have answers for every question about the resurrection. But I'm confident that "in fact Christ has been raised from the dead" (1 Cor 15:20). It is the good news in which we live, die, and are raised to new life. Charles Wesley gave us the words to sing:

> Soar we now where Christ has led, Alleluia!
> Following our exalted Head, Alleluia!
> Made like him, like him we rise, Alleluia!
> Ours the cross, the grave, the skies, Alleluia![16]

---

15. Moltmann, *In the End*, 100.
16. Young, *United Methodist Hymnal*, 302.

6

Becoming the Hope

"All were united in their devotion to prayer . . . including Mary the mother of Jesus." (Acts 1:14)

How did I miss her? Why was I surprised to find Mary waiting with Jesus' followers during the fifty days between Easter and Pentecost? Jerusha Matsen Neal said she found comfort in Luke's decision to place Mary in the upper room. She wrote, "After all she goes through, after all the ways this small community fails the Jesus she loves, she is still there, committed to them, loving them, listening for the Spirit with them."[1] They stayed together, perhaps because of hope, probably because of fear. I assume that despite their experiences with their risen Lord, the ghastly memory of the way Jesus died still haunted them. They wondered what would become of everything they had seen, heard, and hoped during their time with Jesus. They wondered what might come next. Most of all, they wondered what would become of them.

How do you picture Mary during this time of waiting? In classic paintings of Mary at Pentecost, she appears to be eternally young, always glowing with a beatific warmth, never aging, never losing her virginal purity. But over three decades have passed since the day she said "yes" to Gabriel's invitation. Her life was never

---

1. Personal correspondence.

easy. Along the way, she discovered what Simeon meant when he predicted that being Jesus' mother would break her heart. Only a few weeks have passed since she experienced the horror of the crucifixion and the surprise of the resurrection. In her soul-wrenching grief and relentless hope, Mary must have been at the center of the group of disoriented disciples Luke identified as "the family of believers" (Luke 1:15). I imagine her presence among Jesus' followers in ways that are similar to John Steinbeck's description of Ma Joad in *The Grapes of Wrath*.

> Her full face was not soft; it was controlled, kindly. Her hazel eyes seemed to have experienced all possible tragedy and to have mounted pain and suffering like steps into a high calm and a superhuman understanding. She seemed to know, to accept, to welcome her position, the citadel of the family, the strong place that could not be taken. . . . It was her trait to build up laughter out of inadequate materials. . . . From her great and humble position in the family she had taken dignity and a clean calm beauty. . . . She seemed to know that if she swayed the family shook, and if she ever really deeply wavered or despaired the family would fall.[2]

I found Mary's likeness in the mother whose searing grief and unrelenting faith held her family together after her son's suicide. I experienced Mary's quiet courage in the young mother whose elementary-school-age daughter, afflicted by a terminal disease, died in her arms. I heard Mary's ability to "build up laughter out of inadequate materials" in the mother who rediscovered her laughter sometime after she buried her teenage son as the result of a tragic car accident. I felt her spiritual maturity in the grandmother who waited beside her son's hospital bed for the machines to be turned off and went immediately to focus her attention on her young grandsons. I see her in the determination of mothers who cradle their children in underground shelters in Kiev and who bury their children because of our culture's insane gun violence. Given all Mary had been through, it's no surprise that she became

---

2. Steinbeck, *Grapes of Wrath*, 95–96.

a center of love and devotion from the earliest days of the Christian tradition.

In whatever way you picture Mary, she was with Jesus' followers during the forty days during which the risen Christ instructed his disciples, showed them he was alive, ate with them, spoke about the kingdom of God, and told them to wait in Jerusalem for the coming of the Holy Spirit (Acts 1:2–6). She evidently joined them when Jesus led them to the Mount of Olives where "he was lifted up and a cloud took him out of their sight" (Acts 1:9). The scene is reminiscent of the way "Elijah went up by a whirlwind into heaven" (2 Kgs 2:11) when his work was completed.

Don't ask me to explain the astrophysics of the Ascension! I remember feeling the ground shake at Cape Kennedy as we watched the space shuttle lift off. I didn't need to understand the thrust of the rockets to feel their power and to stand in awe-stricken amazement at the reality of something that was beyond my ability to explain. Similarly, whatever the disciples experienced on the Mount of Olives was beyond their explanation. One of my mentors said the church has never worried about whether the Ascension story is scientifically factual but has always claimed it is eternally true. Long after leaving the cosmology of a three-storied universe behind, we still know the power of the biblical imagery. We say the sun rises and sets, though we know it does nothing of the kind. We know how it feels to be "up" or to be "down." We know when someone is "on top of things," or "on the way up," and we know when things are "going downhill." (Although I don't appreciate those who speak negatively about "going south" after living here for most of my life!)

Are we crossing our fingers behind our backs when we affirm the creed? "For us and our salvation he came down from heaven. . . . He ascended into heaven and is seated at the right hand of the Father. He will come again in glory." How do we understand the "up" and "down" language in the Bible? What are we celebrating on Ascension Day?

One option is to see the Ascension story through the lens of the royal imagery in the Psalms. The lectionary Scripture readings for celebration of the Ascension include Psalm 68 in which the writer envisions "the procession of my God, my king, into the sanctuary" (Ps 68:24).

> Let God rise up;
> > let his enemies scatter;
> > > let those who hate him
> > > > run scared before him! . . .
> But let the righteous be glad
> > and celebrate before God.
> > > Let them rejoice with gladness!
> Sing to God! Sing praises to his name!
> > Exalt the one who rides the clouds!
> > The Lord is his name.
> > > Celebrate before him!
>
> Sing to God, all kingdoms of the earth!
> > Sing praises to my Lord.
> Sing to the one who rides through heaven,
> > the most ancient heaven. (Ps 68:1–4, 32–33)

The royal imagery continues to be alive with us long after the global era of royal power passed. I was working on this chapter when the same American citizens who joyfully celebrate their freedom from British rule on July 4 were entranced by the coronation of King Charles III. When he "ascended" to the throne and sat down on the Stone of Scone, we saw Charles become what he was becoming across the seventy-four years of his life. Even though the British monarchy is largely a symbolic reminder of a gilded past nevertheless stained by centuries of slavery, domination, and the plundering of resources on almost every continent, it still holds the grandeur of tradition and helps define the identity of citizens of the UK. For many of the British people, the coronation events apparently lifted their vision of who they are above the day-to-day conflict and chaos of their politics.

In a much more profound and expansively universal way, the Ascension raises our spirits to see Christ "lifted up" above the flattened, ground-level, mundane world in which we normally live. It's more about theology than astrophysics. It marks the culmination of the mission Jesus came to accomplish. The one who "came down" to be with us, who lived, died, and rose from death among us has completed the saving work for which God sent him. Wesley's Easter hymn proclaims, "Love's redeeming work is done!" Now, he is "taken up" to be one with the God who sent him, leaving his followers with the promise of the Spirit who will "come down" to live in and through them. The Ascension story also points toward that day when "He shall come again in glory."

I learned the truth of the Ascension as a teenager growing up in the Methodist Youth Fellowship when its motto was "Christ Above All." I remember seeing those words carved on the front of the pulpit at the Methodist youth camp. The Ascension declares Christ is above every boundary of nation, race, class, and culture. He takes priority over all our human commitments, relationships, or institutions. He is "far above every ruler and authority and power and angelic power, any power that might be named not only now but in the future" (Eph 1:21). In his life, death, and resurrection we see the creating, self-giving love that is at the heart of the universe. The Ascension confirms the way revealed in Jesus to be the way the Almighty God is at work to redeem, reign, and rule the whole of creation. And Jesus' mother was there to see it all!

"They were all together in one place." (Acts 2:1)

Mary was with Jesus' followers when they came down from the Mount of Olives and returned to Jerusalem. Luke reports, "The family of believers was a company of about one hundred twenty persons" (Acts 1:15). That's a large "family!" I'm sure there were differences and disagreements among them. As days dragged by, they must have driven each other crazy. And yet, they remained together because they were bound to each other in their shared grief over the loss of what they had been and their questions about what they would become.

In our highly individualized culture, we often tend to describe our relationship with Christ in narrowly individualized terms. We act as if the creed says Christ came down "for *me* and *my* salvation" rather than for "*us* and *our* salvation." I can easily forget *my* salvation is bound up in *our* salvation and in God's salvation of this whole broken and bruised creation.

There is a profoundly personal element to the Christian faith. No one can be baptized or receive the bread and cup for me. No one can follow Christ for me or practice for me the spiritual disciplines by which Christ is born again in me. But the biblical vision of God's salvation reaches far beyond my individualized experience. I remember an aging preacher who said if salvation doesn't begin in me, it doesn't begin; but if salvation ends in me, it ends. We are engaged in something far larger than our individual self-interest. We are saved with and for others. When we follow Jesus, he draws us into God's process of salvation, which is beyond everything we can imagine, stretching across all of time and space.

Archbishop Desmond Tutu, the spiritual leader of the struggle against apartheid in South Africa, was the living expression of the ancient African tradition of *ubuntu*. The term declares, "I am who I am because of who we are." It affirms that we are inextricably bound together in the intricate web of our humanity. *Ubuntu* emerges from a deep appreciation of tradition and leads to a transformative awareness that individual actions today reflect the past and will have consequences in the future. It becomes the context in which we find our place in the universe.

In the upper room, the "family of disciples" did not wait for the coming of the Holy Spirit as solitary saints or isolated individuals. The fact that they waited together led me to some intriguing questions:

- What might have happened to the rest of the "family" if Mary had withdrawn in solitary grief?
- How much more depressing would the memory of the crucifixion have been if each of them were hiding alone?
- How much more confusing would the empty tomb be if they were not experiencing the presence of the risen Christ together?

- How much more hopeless would the days from the resurrection to the Pentecost have been if each person had faced them on their own?
- What would they have missed and what would they never have become had they not been "all together in one place"? (Acts 2:1)

The life of the early Christian community underscores the truth that hope springs from and is sustained by being in community. We find hope in being with people we love and who love us. We see the emerging likeness of Christ in ourselves when we see ourselves through the eyes of people we trust. The memories of my visits to the Abbey of Gethsemani where Thomas Merton spent his life remind me that even monks whose lives are committed to silence and prayer are bound together in the community of their work and worship. Like those first Christians, we need to be with each other if we are to become all God intends for us to be.

The US Surgeon General recently released a major report on "Our Epidemic of Loneliness and Isolation." The study found that even before the COVID-19 pandemic, about half of US adults reported measurable levels of loneliness. The numbers have only increased in the years since then. The report warned that loneliness is as damaging to our health as smoking or obesity. The effects of the lack of human connection include an increased risk of heart disease, stroke, and dementia for older adults. It can contribute to the risk of suicide and drug abuse for teenagers.[3]

The report confirmed the biblical truth that even our physical bodies need human connection. On the opening pages of Scripture, the Creator declares, "It's not good that the human is alone" (Gen 2:18). The Bible ends with John's vision of "a great crowd that no one could number . . . from every nation, tribe, people, and language . . . standing before the throne and before the Lamb" (Rev 7:9). The Old Testament is the saga of God's relationship with the covenant community of Israel. The New Testament draws us into the community of Christ's followers. From cover to cover, through obedience and failure, unity and division, joy and pain, life and

3. Egan, "US Surgeon General."

death, the Bible affirms we are created to live in connection with each other, with the rest of creation, and with God.

Our identity as disciples of Christ means living in an imperfect community with other imperfect disciples. I remember hearing E. Stanley Jones say that everyone who belongs to Christ belongs to everyone who belongs to Christ. Dietrich Bonhoeffer declared, "Whoever seeks to become a new human being individually cannot succeed."[4] More recently, popular Christian author Rachel Held Evans concluded, "Like it or not, you can't be a Christian on your own. Following Jesus is a group activity, and from the beginning it's been a messy one."[5]

I thank God for every way I experience the Spirit's presence in profoundly personal ways in the daily discipline of prayer and reflection on Scripture, sitting alone in the silence of a Kentucky monastery, or watching the sun rise over the Great Smoky Mountains. But nothing I experience alone compares to the presence of the living Christ in community with other disciples; in the laughter, intimacy, and tears of long-term friendships; in the rich diversity of fellowship with faithful disciples from around the world; in congregational worship in magnificent cathedrals or in informal settlements in South Africa. It's no surprise to me that the writer of Hebrews said, "Don't stop meeting together with other believers, which some people have gotten into the habit of doing. Instead, encourage each other, especially as you see the day drawing near" (Heb 10:25).

We are created for and called to life together. This truth caused John Wesley to assert that the phrase "holy solitaries" was "no more consistent with the gospel than Holy Adulterers." He was convinced "the gospel of Christ knows of no religion, but social; no holiness but social holiness. Faith working by love, is the length and breadth and depth and height of Christian perfection."[6]

---

4. Bonhoeffer, *Discipleship*, 219.
5. Evans, *Inspired*, 206.
6. Manskar, "Social Holiness," para. 7.

Surprised by Mary

"A fierce wind... and flames of fire." (Acts 2:2–3)

Mary was in the upper room when the Holy Spirit came "like the howling of a fierce wind.... They saw what seemed to be individual flames of fire alighting on each one of them. They were all filled with the Holy Spirit" (Acts 2:2–4).

Luke drew vivid metaphors from nature and from Scripture to describe an experience that was beyond explanation. The best he could do was to say, "It was like..." Wind can be a gentle breeze that rustles through the palm fronds on a hot summer day, and it can sweep in from the Gulf of Mexico with the force of a hurricane. Fire can be the warmth of the cabin fireplace on a cool evening in the mountains, and it can be a California wildfire wiping out a community. They are two of the most powerful metaphors in Scripture for the ways people experience the Spirit. The breath of God that blew over chaos to form creation and the unquenchable fire in which Moses heard God's call to liberate the people were the only way Luke could describe their experience on Pentecost.

Jesus' followers prepared for the coming of the Holy Spirit through their life together and the discipline of prayer, but the wind and fire still came as a room-shaking surprise. Their example teaches us we can prepare for Spirit's presence through time-tested spiritual disciplines, but we cannot cause, predict, or control the way the Spirit will be at work through our lives or in our world, except to say that everything the Spirit does is consistent with what we see in Jesus (John 14:25–6). Lauren Winner reminds us, "Sometimes the flames leap and dance, not because of anything you did. Sometimes the flame dies, despite everything you did."[7]

Jesus said, "God's Spirit blows wherever it wishes. You hear its sound, but you don't know where it comes from or where it is going" (John 3:8). We do not cause the wind and fire of the Spirit to come among us by our preparation, but we are unlikely to experience the Spirit's movement if we are not prepared for it. We may not know where the Spirit comes from or be able to predict where

---

7. Winner, *Wearing God*, 209.

the Spirit will go, but we can see the effect in the lives of those who experience it.

The importance of the Pentecost story is not contained in the details of how the Spirit came, as if the disciples could have recorded the velocity of the wind or the temperature of the fire. Rather, we see the importance of what happened that day in what Jesus' followers became because of it. The wind of the Spirit swept them out of the safe, narrow confines of the place where they were hiding into a more expansive world they would never have seen or known. The fire of the Spirit set their hearts ablaze with the flaming passion Jeremiah said was like a fire in his bones that he could not extinguish (Jer 20:9). The Spirit who descended on Jesus at his baptism and sent him "to preach good news to the poor, to proclaim release to the prisoners and recovery of sight to the blind, to liberate the oppressed, and to proclaim the year of the Lord's favor" (Luke 4:18–19) was now sending his disciples in the same way.

By the power of the Holy Spirit, ordinary men and women became something they otherwise would never have become—the finite, imperfect, ordinary witnesses of the infinite, perfect, extraordinary love of God revealed in Christ. They became the people through whom Jesus was born again into the world. Thirteen centuries later, St. Francis of Assisi said, "We are His mothers when we bear Him in our heart and in our body through pure love and bring Him forth by holy work which might shine as an example to others."[8]

The same Holy Spirit who overshadowed Mary in the beginning of her story was present with Maria Skobtsova in the twentieth century. She is remembered as Mother Maria or St. Mary of Paris. Maria became a nun only after her bishop assured her that she could live in the world rather than in a monastery. She opened a house for refugees in Paris which became a safe place for Jews after the Nazis invaded France. Because she took part in the resistance, the authorities sent her to the concentration camp in Ravensbrück, Germany, where she went to the gas chamber on Holy Saturday, 1945. Prior to her arrest, Maria had written,

---

8. Francis, *Writings*, para. 18.

> It would be a great lie to tell searching souls: "Go to church, because there you will find peace." The opposite is true. [The church] tells those who are at peace and asleep: "Go to church, because there you will feel real alarm for your sins, about your perdition, about the world's sins and perdition. There you will feel an unappeasable hunger for Christ's truth. There instead of lukewarm you will become ardent, instead of pacified you will become alarmed, instead of learning the wisdom of this world you will become foolish in Christ."[9]

The readers of this book may not be called to a life that leads to literal martyrdom, though that is ultimately what happened to many of the disciples who gathered in that upper room. It still happens in parts of our world where people are banned for converting to Christianity, imprisoned, or executed for confronting the powers of oppression and lies with the word of liberation and truth. Some experience a more subtle form of martyrdom when they are shunned or silenced for standing up for their convictions; lose their livelihood because of religious, racial, or sexual bias; or suffer the effects of racism, sexism, or violence. The book of Acts confirms that the Holy Spirit does not primarily come to make our lives a little more manageable; to guarantee health, wealth, and happiness; or to give us the life we've always wanted. The gifts of the Spirit are given to empower us to be the presence of Christ in a confusing, conflicted, and unpredictable world. The wind of the Spirit may send us to places we would not otherwise go. The fire of the Spirit may energize us to do things we would not otherwise do. I've seen the fire and wind of the Spirit in:

- ordinary people like the women from a comfortable, upper-class neighborhood who drive for Meals on Wheels and have become friends with people in the poorest neighborhood in our city.
- persistent people who are not satisfied with "thoughts and prayers" in the aftermath of our weekly mass shootings and

---

9. Skobtsova, "Quotes Taken from *Mother Maria*," para. 1.

- who work relentlessly for reasonable gun safety measures against the seemingly insurmountable opposition in our legislature.
- volunteers who serve meals, offer haircuts, provide dental care, and give legal assistance to people who are homeless.
- a young attorney who turned down a lucrative opportunity to work in a major law firm to invest his career ensuring legal access for people with developmental disabilities.
- parents who love and affirm their LGBTQ children.
- seminary students who are giving their lives in ministry through the church in a challenging and unpredictable time.
- a small group of successful, upwardly mobile professional men who became the presence of Christ with one group member who fought cancer and survived and with another until he died.

By the Spirit's presence, ordinary people become the extraordinary bearers of hope in a world that sometimes seems hopeless, midwives of love in a world of hate, bringers of joy in a world of pain, and the promise of new life in every place of death.

"We are being transformed into that same image from one degree of glory to the next degree of glory. This comes from the Lord, who is the Spirit." (2 Cor 3:18)

Pentecost is not only a past event we celebrate in church history, as important as that is. The invasive wind and soul-warming fire Mary and the other disciples experienced that day are the ongoing reality of the Holy Spirit at work in the lives of Jesus' followers in every age. The Spirit's continuing task is to transform us from what we have been to what we can become and to shape our living and thinking in ways that are consistent with the way of Christ, "from one degree of glory to the next." Bonhoeffer said, "Christians prove their identity not in what they have become, but by always remaining in the process of becoming."[10] The fire of the Spirit refines, warms, and energizes our hearts. The wind of the Spirit sends us out into the world to be the agents of God's transforming love, peace, and justice.

John Wesley gave his followers a unique way to describe the process by which the Holy Spirit transforms us from one degree to the next. He called it "sanctification" or "Christian perfection." Being "made perfect in love" is the lifelong process by which the Spirit makes us more and more like Jesus. The goal is "holiness" defined by what Jesus named as the greatest commandments. Holiness of heart is our love of God; holiness of life is our love of neighbor.

Wesley named two "means of grace" by which we grow toward perfection in love. The "works of piety" include individual practices of spiritual formation by reading Scripture, prayer, and fasting, along with communal practices of worship centered on the sacraments, accountability to one another, and group Bible study. The "works of mercy" are what one colleague called "the concrete expression of love with skin on it." They include individual practices of doing good works, visiting the sick or those in prison, feeding the hungry, and giving generously to the needs of others along with communal practices of seeking justice, ending oppression and discrimination, and being in ministry with the poor.

If the "means" by which we grow toward perfection sound overwhelming, take heart! We don't reach perfection all at once! The Christian life is not defined by where we have been or what we have accomplished but by the direction in which we are moving. The New Testament Greek word for "perfection" is *telos*. It is the ultimate end, purpose, or goal toward which we grow, and which will be completed in the new life of the resurrection. Although it requires spiritual and personal discipline, we do not grow toward perfection by our human determination or power alone. It's not something we achieve, attain, or earn. It is the result of the transforming presence of the Spirit within us. The Holy Spirit meets us wherever we are and enables us to take the next appropriate step in

---

10. Bonhoeffer, *Sanctorum Communio*, 305.

becoming a person who loves God with all our heart, mind, soul, and strength, and who loves others the way we have been loved by God in Christ. Charles Wesley described the goal toward which the process leads when he taught us to sing:

> Finish, then, thy new creation;
> pure and spotless let us be.
> Let us see thy great salvation
> perfectly restored in thee.
> Changed from glory into glory,
> till in heav'n we take our place,
> till we cast our crowns before thee,
> lost in wonder, love, and praise.[11]

I've never been able to improve on the words of a farmer in the little congregation I served in the fern-growing corner of North Central Florida. When I asked how he was doing, he immediately responded, "Well, Preacher, I'm not the man I used to be, and I'm not yet the man I hope to be, but I'm more the man God wants me to be than I've ever been before." That's Christian perfection! Wesley's questions for every person being ordained in the Methodist tradition apply to every follower of Christ:

> Are you going on to perfection?
> Do you expect to be made perfect in love in this life?
> Are you earnestly striving after it?[12]

"Everyone heard them speaking in their native language." (Acts 2:6)

I'm pretty sure the disciples were just as "surprised and bewildered" as the people who heard them when the Spirit enabled them "to speak in other languages as the Spirit enabled them to speak" (Acts 2:4). I remain bewildered by the linguistics of the story, although I know people who have experienced it. This was not speaking in unintelligible tongues as some parts of the Christian tradition encourage. We can debate whether the Spirit was at work on the

---

11. Young, *United Methodist Hymnal*, 384.
12. Alexander, *Book of Worship*, 720.

speakers' tongues or in the listeners' ears, but Peter's interpretation of the event is unquestionably direct. He announced it as the fulfillment of the promise to the Old Testament prophet Joel.

> I will pour out my Spirit on all people.
>   Your sons and daughters will prophesy.
>   Your young will see visions.
>   Your elders will dream dreams.
>   Even upon my servants, men and women,
>   I will pour out my Spirit in those days,
>   and they will prophesy. (Acts 2:17–18)

Whatever happened that day, it declared the good news that what God did in the life, death, and resurrection of Jesus is for all kinds of people, who speak all kinds of languages, and live in all kinds of places. The same Spirit who "hovered over" chaos to bring forth creation and who "overshadowed" a young woman named Mary who gave birth to the Son of God, was now giving birth to a new creation that would become the living, loving, serving presence of Christ in the world. Jesus was, in fact, being born again through his new body, the church. As surprising and bewildering as it may sound, the life that became flesh through Mary's body is now becoming flesh through his church.

As I reflect on this story and write these words, I am forced to acknowledge again how the church falls short of the Spirit's extravagantly inclusive intention, always with tragic results. Despite what they experienced and proclaimed on Pentecost, the persistent tension in the early church was around who they would include and who they would not. The debate about the need for circumcision divided Peter and Paul. Questions about inclusion created conflict in the churches to which Paul wrote his letters, particularly the church in Corinth. Paul could not have imagined that his eloquent chapter on love would become a staple part of wedding ceremonies (1 Cor 13). He wrote it to inspire church members to live together in ways that demonstrate the love they received from Christ, the love that can overcome differences and become the tangible expression of that love to others.

Becoming the Hope

Across church history, the Holy Spirit has continued to push relentlessly against the human boundaries of tradition, culture, nationality, social status, race, and sexual identity that separate Christ's followers from each other and from the world they are called to serve. We continually fail to live up to Jesus' prayer that with all our unique differences we might all be one, even as he and his Father in heaven are one (John 18:23). Despite major steps forward in my lifetime, the current political polarization has unleashed divisive powers of racism that continue to fester beneath the surface of our highly polished cultural veneer.

On Good Friday, 1963, Martin Luther King Jr. was in solitary confinement in the Birmingham Jail. That same day, a letter from eight prominent white clergy appeared in the *Birmingham News*, which criticized the civil rights movement as being "unwise and untimely." Like Paul writing from a prison cell in Rome or John in exile on Patmos, King wrote his response in the margins of the newspaper and on paper smuggled to him by a secretive jailer. His "Letter from Birmingham Jail" became a foundational document of the Civil Rights Movement. Dr. King addressed the letter with deep disappointment to the church leaders who he had hoped would join the movement for justice. He challenged the white church to live up to its identity as the body of Christ in the present moment.

Writing on the sixtieth anniversary of the release of the letter, King scholar Richard Lischer recommended we read King's words "like a registered letter to which White Christians are required to reply." Dr. King's words continue to call us to rediscover our identity as "a colony of heaven" whose life in the world bears witness to the kingdom vision of life, justice, and wholeness for all people.[13]

Although some of the racial patterns of the Jim Crow era have changed, the challenge still confronts us in increasingly dangerous movements of white supremacy, Nazism, and the ultimate biblical oxymoron "Christian nationalism." The forces of division are as ruthless as they are relentless in pushing back against the movement for diversity, equity, and inclusion.

---

13. Lischer, "King's Letter," paras. 25, 29.

Surprised by Mary

Peter said, "I really am learning that God doesn't show partiality to one group of people over another." (Acts 10:34)

In a similar way, we continue to wrestle with division around the inclusion of LGBTQ Christians in the life and ministry of the church. I have lived with the tension around this question throughout my years of ministry.

I graduated from seminary and entered my first pastoral appointment in 1972. That was the year the General Conference of The United Methodist Church inserted words into the Book of Discipline that define "the practice of homosexuality" as being "incompatible with Christian teaching and tradition."[14] Succeeding General Conferences added prohibitions around marriage and ministry. As a delegate to those Conferences, I supported the incompatibility language until the Spirit confronted me with a choice between loyalty to the old law or life in the law of love in the new creation. The change came as I found myself in the transformative story of Peter's experience on a rooftop in Joppa (Acts 10:1–23).

Peter was waiting for lunch. He was so hungry that he fell into a trance in which he saw a sheet being lowered from heaven, loaded down with animals the Old Testament kosher laws called "unclean." A voice told him, "Kill and eat." But Peter protested, "Absolutely not, Lord! I have never eaten anything impure or unclean!" (It takes some nerve to talk back to the Lord that way!) The voice responded, "Never consider unclean what God has made pure." This happened three times! Then the sheet disappeared leaving Peter "bewildered about the meaning of the vision." But he would soon find out!

Right then, there was a knock at the door. Messengers from a Roman centurion named Cornelius invited Peter to come home with them. Cornelius was a Gentile, just the kind of person a faithful Jew would see as being as unclean as the beasts in the sheet. But in no uncertain terms, the Spirit told Peter, "Don't ask questions; just go with them." Peter went and discovered a house full of people who were waiting for him. He told them, "I am really learning that God

---

14. United Methodist Church, *Book of Discipline*, para. 304.3.

doesn't show partiality to one group over another." As he told them about Jesus, "The Holy Spirit fell on everyone who heard the word." Luke records that "the circumcised believers who had come with Peter were astonished that the gift of the Holy Spirit had been poured out even on the Gentiles" (Acts 10:45). Later, when Peter was called to explain his actions to the apostles in Jerusalem, he said, "If God gave them the same gift he gave us who believed in the Lord Jesus Christ, then who am I? Could I stand in God's way?" (Acts 15:17).

Peter saw the vision and heard the voice, but it was the relationship with Cornelius and his family and friends that changed Peter's life. Relationships often do that! In this, as in so many places, the clarity of one's convictions about a certain subject is often in direct proportion to the distance away from it. I never saw a vision or heard a voice, but my relationships with faithful LGBTQ followers of Christ had a direct impact on my life. Through them, the Spirit moved me toward acceptance and inclusion. I was forced to ask, "If God gave them the same gift he gave me, who am I to stand in God's way?"

I cannot expect everyone to have my Joppa type of experience or to come to the same convictions on the marriage and ordination of LGBTQ persons. I am disappointed that one-time pastoral colleagues feel led to leave The United Methodist Church over this issue. Methodists faced this kind of separation in 1844 when the church divided between north and south over the issue of slavery. Living through our present crisis, I've often asked God in prayer how it is that former mentors and friends, equally faithful disciples who share the same commitment to Scripture and sincerely pray for the Spirit to lead them, end up at such divergent places. I have not found an adequate answer to that question. I concluded a conversation with a disaffiliating colleague by saying, "One day we will all be gathered around the throne in heaven, and the only thing we will be able to say will be, 'Lord, we were doing the best we knew how to do by being as faithful as we knew how to be.'"

I'm sometimes tempted to agree with the cynic who compared the church to Noah's ark. He said the only way to stand the stench on the inside is fear of the storm on the outside. But despite its weaknesses, failures, and tragic compromises with the economic, social, and political powers of the world around us, I still believe "the Church is of God, and will be preserved to the end of time." I still believe "all of every age and station, stand in need of the means of grace which it alone supplies."[15] With New Testament scholar and authority on the early church, C. Kavin Rowe, I know "Christians live in the time where they serve Jesus in a still-fallen world that is being newly created now, await his final return, and hope for the eternal healing of all that is."[16] I still believe that when we are at our best, this imperfect, inadequate, and sometimes insufferable body we call "church" is the living, breathing, life-giving Body of Christ in this world.

I am who I am as an imperfect follower of Jesus because imperfect people in an imperfect church have been who they have been throughout history and in my life. In the brokenness of our past and the tensions of the present, I find life-giving examples of people and communities who are continuously becoming the flesh and blood body of the one who became flesh through Mary. They model the hope the prophets imagined in the Old Testament. They hold onto the promise Gabriel announced to a girl in Nazareth. They share the joy the angels celebrated in Bethlehem. They follow the self-giving love revealed at the cross. They experience the surprise the women discovered at the empty tomb. They participate in the new creation the Holy Spirit rebirthed on Pentecost. They are "becomers" in a body that is always becoming more like the one whose life, death, and resurrection gave them new birth.

Christianity's greatest surprise is that by the power of the Holy Spirit, any of us, all of us, can surprise the world by becoming the ordinary people through whom the extraordinary presence of Christ is born again!

---

15. Young, *United Methodist Hymnal*, 45.
16. Rowe, *Christianity's Surprise*, 3.

Epilogue

BEATING THE BEAST

"The Woman Clothed with the Sun" (Rev 12:1–17)

Every enquiring mind wants to know what became of Mary. Unfortunately, no one knows. Despite the plethora of legends, liturgical traditions, and divergent theologies that have accumulated around her story, the New Testament is frustratingly silent after her appearance on Pentecost. Aside from Jesus' commitment of his mother into John's care, there is no biblical information about where she lived or when she died. The concept of Mary's "bodily assumption"—the belief that "having completed the course of her earthly life, [she] was assumed body and soul into heavenly glory"—goes back in oral tradition to the early church fathers. It became official doctrine in the Roman Catholic Church when Pope Pius XII declared it to be "a divinely revealed dogma" in 1950.

While I respect the devotion to Mary out of which Roman Catholic Mariology developed, you've already discovered that I see Mary as a very ordinary human being like any of us through whose very human body "the Word became flesh and made his home among us" (John 1:14). It's enough for me to assume that living as one of us, she died as one of us, and lives again as we will all live again in the new life of the resurrection.

I was, however, surprised by one more glimpse of Mary in Scripture. It appears on the last pages of the New Testament in the book of Revelation.

Surprised by Mary

"I, John, your brother who shares with you in the hardship, kingdom, and endurance . . . was in a Spirit-inspired trance on the Lord's Day." (Rev 1:9–10)

I often introduce study groups to Revelation by saying, "If you liked *Star Wars*, you'll love Revelation!" They are similar apocalyptic literature that portrays the struggle between good and evil in spectacular visions and dramatic stories. If George Lucas is not your style, you might think of J. R. R. Tolkien's *The Lord of the Rings* or C. S. Lewis's *The Chronicles of Narnia*.

The writer of Revelation was a political prisoner on the Island of Patmos, like Nelson Mandela imprisoned on Robben Island. I picture John, like Mandela, looking out over the windswept water that separated him from the mainland. It was the Lord's Day, the day his colleagues across the water were celebrating the resurrection. While he was in prayer, John had a dream. Like all our dreams, John's dreams are not static or frozen but fold into each other like images in a kaleidoscope. When we wake up, some of those dreams are crystal clear, while others fade into the deep recesses of our minds.

If we take John's dreams literally or attempt to put them on a calendar of future events, we'll have a hard time taking them seriously and potentially miss the point along the way. But if we hear his words being read aloud the way he intended (Rev 1:3) in the context in which he wrote them; if we allow his visions to come alive in our imagination; if we remember Luke Skywalker's battle with the Empire, Frodo Baggins's struggle against the power of darkness, or the Pevensie children making their way through Narnia, we can discover why Lewis wrote on the final pages of the *Chronicles*, "The further up and further in you go, the bigger everything gets. The inside is larger than the outside."[1]

When we read Revelation, we're reading someone else's mail. The book is addressed to real people in real places who are confronted by very real powers of evil, oppression, suffering, and death. John sent it to seven congregations of Christians in

---

1. Lewis, *Last Battle*, 180.

Epilogue

modern-day Turkey who were under the domination of the Roman Empire. John wrote in coded language to protect his readers from accusations of treason. Many of its images come from the Old Testament, which is quoted more often in Revelation than in any other book in the New Testament.

All of which takes us to Revelation 12–13. If you take time to read it, you may be surprised by who you find!

"A great sign appeared in heaven: a woman clothed with the sun, with the moon under her feet and a crown of twelve stars on her head." (Rev 12:1)

The woman in John's dream "was pregnant, and she cried out because she was in labor, in pain from giving birth." John's dream suddenly became a nightmare with the appearance of a horrifying, red dragon waiting to devour her child as soon as it was born. But when the baby arrived, it was "snatched up by God and taken to his throne" (Rev 12:1–5). John's first readers may have remembered a possible connection to Moses, born under the threat of death in Egypt, but rescued in his floating cradle. They certainly thought of Mary giving birth to Jesus and escaping Herod's murderous order. Then, in a conflict equal to anything Lucas imagined, the beast is finally defeated by the archangel Michael and is tossed out of heaven.

Dreams usually arise from something we have known or experienced. John's readers would have been familiar with the ancient myths of a royal or divine child who escaped from a superhuman enemy at birth. In the Greek version, the goddess Leto was with child by Zeus and was pursued by the dragon Python. She escaped to the sea god, Poseidon, who took her to an island where she gave birth to Apollo. In Egyptian mythology, Isis, the mother of the gods, was pursued by a dragon but fled to an island where she raised her son and slew the dragon.[2]

It does not undermine the inspiration of Scripture to see the way the Spirit used images from the surrounding culture to

---

2. Laymon, *Interpreters One-Volume Commentary*, 959.

provide a subversive word of hope for Christians facing persecution. Because a faithful reading of Revelation requires a Spirit-inspired imagination, try imagining this.

Imagine the writer of Revelation was John, the "beloved disciple" to whom Jesus entrusted his mother. Imagine that John cared for her until she died. As Mary grew older, she repeated more often (the way older adults often do!) her stories of Jesus' birth and childhood. Perhaps she would wake up in the night, shaking in fear as she relived the frantic escape to Egypt to protect her infant son from Herod's slaughter. John listened and calmed her fears with the reminder that Jesus survived Herod's threat and ultimately overcame the power of death.

Sometime later, imagine John as an old man, alone on Patmos, writing to his fellow Christians who were living in fear of being devoured by the powers of Rome. He dreamed of Mary giving birth to the son who would defeat the dragon of evil. He used the myths of the pagan culture to paint a subversive narrative of the way Mary's Son would ultimately become "the male child who is to rule all the nations" (Rev 12:5). When the dragon was defeated, John heard a loud voice from heaven:

> Now the salvation and power and kingdom of our God,
>   and the authority of his Christ have come.
> The accuser of our brothers and sisters,
>   who accuses them day and night before our God,
>   has been thrown down.
> They gained the victory over him on account of the blood of the Lamb
>   and the word of their witness. (Rev 12:10-11)

Perhaps when John penned these words, he heard the echo of Mary's song at the beginning of her story.

> The Lord has shown strength with his arm.
>   He has scattered those with arrogant thoughts and proud inclination.
>   He has pulled the powerful down from their thrones
>   and lifted up the lowly. . . .
> He has come to the aid of his servant Israel,

Epilogue

> remembering his mercy,
> just as he promised to our ancestors,
> to Abraham and to Abraham's descendants forever.
>
> (Luke 1:51–55)

There is far more color, confusion, and complexity to John's spectacular visions than can be summarized in one scene, just as there is more to Frodo's long and arduous journey to destroy the ring than could ever be captured in one chapter of Tolkien's story. The risks, conflicts, defeats, and failures along the way were a daily reality for the people who first heard John's words. But the struggle is set in the context of John's relentless confidence in how the story will end. He declares it in the opening verses of the book.

> Look, he is coming with the clouds! Every eye will see him, including those who pierced him, and all the tribes of the earth will mourn because of him. This is so. Amen. "I am the Alpha and the Omega," says the Lord God, "the one who is and was and is coming, the Almighty." (Rev 1:7–8)

Imagine being among a small group of Christians hiding in fear of the almost inevitable knock on the door that might take us to the Coliseum. Imagine the way John's vision would energize our hope and strengthen our endurance. Putting us into the picture, Eugene Peterson wrote, "St. John's imagination is adrenaline to us of little faith, and we are again dauntless, unimpressed by dragon bluster, sure of God's preservation. The child survives, salvation is assured."[3] We find the courage to face whatever the "dragon" can do to us with the assurance that although evil is finite, it is not final. Although oppression, suffering, and death are real, they are not the ultimate reality.

We heard this confidence when Martin Luther King Jr. promised the sanitation workers in Memphis that although he might not make it to the destination, they would reach the Promised Land. We saw it during the struggle against Apartheid in South Africa. A reporter recently asked Peter Storey, who led the South

---

3. Peterson, *Reversed Thunder*, 121.

African Methodists through the struggle, "What's your advice about sustaining justice movements when oppression feels overwhelming and insurmountable?" Looking back on his decades of experience, he replied, "Part of it is knowing how the book ends. Desmond Tutu, when things looked totally hopeless, would say to the regime, 'Why don't you join the winning side?'"[4]

"I saw a new heaven and a new earth." (Rev 21:1)

Mary makes her appearance half-way through John's dream that reaches its grand finale in chapter 21. It is John's stunningly beautiful vision of the fulfillment of God's redeeming purpose. He saw a newly redeemed creation in which the sea no longer separated him from his fellow Christians. Looking toward the mainland as the sun broke through the early morning mist, he imagined "the holy city, New Jerusalem, coming down out of heaven from God." It would be nothing less than God taking up residence with his people on earth. "Death will be no more. There will be no mourning, crying, or pain anymore, for the former things have passed away." John heard the One who defeated the Satanic beast declare, "Look! I'm making all things new" (Rev 21:4–5). John Wesley summarized the vision when he wrote:

> The whole brute creation will then, undoubtedly, be restored, not only to the vigour, strength and sweetness which they had at the creation but to a far higher degree of each than they ever enjoyed.[5]

That's a hopeful vision of the future that can enable those who believe it to "be strengthened by the Lord and his powerful strength." Knowing "we aren't fighting against human enemies but against rulers, authorities, forces of cosmic darkness, and spiritual powers of evil," we can be strengthened to "stand [our] ground on the evil day and after [we] have done everything possible to still stand" (Eph 6:10–13).

4. Faith & Leadership, "Peter Storey," para. 20.
5. Wesley, "General Deliverance," para. 22.

Epilogue

It's also a vision that calls for our participation. When we pray for God's kingdom to come and God's will to be done on earth as it is in heaven, we are praying for a vision we are confident God will fulfill in the future to become a reality in the present through us. We are not praying for "pie in the sky by and by," but for God's vision of the world as it will one day be—a world ruled by justice, compassion, and peace that looks like the world Jesus described and the way Jesus lived—to become a reality through us right here, right now.

C. S. Lewis captured the spirit of John's words in one of his most memorable sentences: "Enemy-occupied territory—that is what this world is. Christianity is the story of how the rightful king has landed, you might say landed in disguise, and is calling us to take part in a great campaign of sabotage."[6] Looking toward the day John imagined, Lewis also offered a challenge:

> When the author walks on the stage the play is over.... What is the good of saying you are on His side then, when you see the whole natural universe melting away like a dream and something else—something it never entered your head to conceive—comes crashing in.... That will not be the time for choosing.... Now, today, this moment, is our chance to choose the right side.[7]

"I looked, and there was a great crowd that no one could number." (Rev 7:9)

Mary had one more surprise waiting for me. As I neared the completion of this book, I discovered a tradition dating back to at least the fifth century. It says that the disciples were miraculously gathered from wherever they were in the world to be present at Mary's death.

Caravaggio painted that idea on canvas in *The Death of the Virgin* (1601–6). It was a time when belief in the Assumption

---

6. Lewis, *Mere Christianity*, 51.

7. Lewis, *Mere Christianity*, 66.

of Mary was gaining ground. In contrast to the excessive piety of traditional religious art, Caravaggio captured the earthy reality of ordinary, human death. Mary's lifeless face is pale, her feet are swollen, and her arm hangs limp on the side of the bed. The apostles, including Mary Magdalene, surround Mary's bed, hiding their tears or staring in silent grief.

The painting was rejected by priests who thought it was unfit for their chapel. They were offended by the reality of Mary's lifeless body and by the possibility that the artist used a prostitute, perhaps his mistress, as his model for Mary. In contrast to the priests, I am intrigued by the artist's honesty about death and by the suggestion that even the artist's mistress was not beyond the reach of the love that became flesh through Mary.

Although there is no factual basis for the scene, there is a spiritual sense in which I believe it is true. In ways I would not attempt to explain, I believe the people who were closest to her son were with Mary in that moment, just as surely as they were "all together in one place" on Pentecost. Can you imagine a more beautiful image for the end of her story?

Both Tolkien and Lewis conclude their epic stories with the unexpected reunion of all the people who participated in the struggle along the way. John's vision is structured around spectacular scenes of the throngs of heaven gathered around the throne, including the "people [who] have come out of great hardship" (Rev 7:14). And every time we affirm the creed, we declare our belief in the "communion of the saints."

So, why not imagine in a way that goes beyond the narrow boundaries of human space and time, they were all there when Mary crossed over from this life into the new life of the resurrection? Why not imagine the final scene of Mary's story the way John Bunyan imagined the death of Mr. Valiant-for-Truth in *The Pilgrim's Progress?*

> When the day that he must go hence was come, many accompanied him to the river-side; into which as he went, he said, "Death, where is thy sting?" And as he went down deeper, he said, "Grave, where is thy victory?" So

Epilogue

he passed over; and all the trumpets sounded for him on the other side.[8]

Thinking about Caravaggio's painting of Mary's death led me to remember all the people who, in ways I cannot explain, will surround me in the hour of my passing. As I look back across my life, I am amazed by the faithful family members, colleagues, and friends who have encouraged, guided, challenged, and sometimes frustrated me along the way. Their presence is an ongoing gift of grace far beyond anything I ever earned or deserved. I am who I am because they are who they are in my life.

- Why wouldn't I expect that those who have accompanied me through my life will also accompany me to the Riverside?
- How could I not believe that the love and friendship we have shared together in this life will go with me through death into the new life of the resurrection?
- Why would I ever think that I will be alone when I hear the trumpets on the other side?
- Why not trust that the old gospel hymn got it right in singing, "When we all get to heaven, what a day of rejoicing it will be"?

John began his book with a blessing, "Blessed are those who hear and who keep what is written" (Rev 1:3, NRSV). I cannot think of a better way to conclude this book than to reaffirm the words with which Mary's story began:

> Hail Mary,
> Full of Grace,
> The Lord is with thee.
> Blessed art thou among women,
> and blessed is the fruit
> of thy womb, Jesus.

And blessed are all those who are surprised to discover that the Christ who was born through Mary is being born again through them! Amen!

8. Bunyan, *Pilgrim's Progress*, 285.

Bibliography

Abuelas de Plaza de Mayo. "History of Abuelas de Plaza de Mayo." Accessed May 11, 2023. https://www.globalministries.org/partner/lac_partners_abuelas_de_plaza_de_mayo/.

Adler, Margot. "Peace Activist William Sloane Coffin Dies at 81." *NPR Morning Edition*, April 13, 2006. https://www.npr.org/2006/04/13/5339877/peace-activist-william-sloane-coffin-dies-at-81.

Alexander, Neil, ed. *The United Methodist Book of Worship*. Nashville: Abingdon, 1992.

Armstrong, Karen. *The Spiral Staircase: My Climb Out of Darkness*. New York: Anchor, 2004.

Bass, Diana Butler. "Sunday Musings." *The Cottage*, March 5, 2023. https://dianabutlerbass.substack.com/p/sunday-musings-81d?utm_source=substack&utm_medium=email.

Bochen, Christine M., ed. *Thomas Merton: Essential Writings*. Maryknoll, NY: Orbis, 2000.

Bonhoeffer, Dietrich. *Discipleship*. Translated by Barbara Green and Reinhard Krauss. Dietrich Bonhoeffer Works 4. Minneapolis: Fortress, 1998.

———. *Life Together and Prayerbook of the Bible*. Translated by Daniel W. Bloesch and James H. Burtness. Dietrich Bonhoeffer Works 5. Minneapolis: Fortress, 1998.

———. *Sanctorum Communio*. Translated by Reinhard Krauss and Nancy Lukens. Dietrich Bonhoeffer Works 1. Minneapolis: Fortress, 1998.

Bowler, Kate. *No Cure for Being Human (And Other Truths I Need to Hear)*. New York: Random House, 2021.

Brendlinger, Irv A. *Social Justice Through the Eyes of Wesley*. Ontario: Josh Press, 2006.

Buechner, Frederick. *Telling the Truth: The Gospel as Tragedy, Comedy & Fairy Tale*. New York: Harper & Row, 1977.

———. *Wishful Thinking*. New York: Harper & Row, 1973.

Bunyan, John. *The Pilgrim's Progress*. Grand Rapids: Zondervan, 1967.

Bibliography

Byassee, Jason. "What about Mary? Protestants and Marian Devotion." *The Christian Century*, December 14, 2004. https://www.christiancentury.org/article/2004-12/what-about-mary.

Chilcote, Paul. *The Quest for Love Divine*. Eugene, OR: Cascade, 2022.

Chubkoc, Oleksandr. "A Russian Missile, a Sudden Death, and Unspeakable Grief." *The New York Times*, December 15, 2022. https://www.nytimes.com/2022/12/15/world/europe/missile-attack-kherson-ukraine-photos.html.

Coffin, William Sloane. *Letters to a Young Doubter*. Louisville: Westminster John Knox, 2005.

———. *A Passion for the Possible: A Message to U.S. Churches*. Louisville: Westminster John Knox, 1993.

Cone, James H. *The Cross and the Lynching Tree*. Maryknoll, NY: Orbis, 2017.

Davis, Ellen F. *Getting Involved with God*. Cambridge: Cowley, 2001.

deVega, Magrey. "How Jesus Learned Obedience." *Midweek Message*, March 23, 2023. https://hydeparkumc.org/how-jesus-learned-obedience/.

Dickens, Charles. *A Christmas Carol*. http://www.authorama.com/a-christmas-carol-6.html.

Eckhart, Meister. "Be Mothers of God." Catholic Store Room, n.d. http://www.catholicstoreroom.com/category/quotes/quote-author/meister-eckhart-1260–1328/.

Egan, Emma. "US Surgeon General Calls for Action Regarding the Ongoing 'Epidemic of Loneliness and Isolation.'" *ABC News*, May 2, 2023. https://abcnews.go.com/Health/us-surgeon-general-calls-action-ongoing-epidemic-loneliness/story?id=98988970.

Evans, Rachel Held. *Inspired: Slaying Giants, Walking on Water, and Loving the Bible Again*. Nashville: Nelson, 2018.

Faith & Leadership. "Peter Storey: Is the Church Here for the World or Itself?" January 20, 2023. https://faithandleadership.com/peter-storey-the-church-here-the-world-or-itself.

Foster, Richard J., and James Bryan Smith, eds. *Devotional Classics: Selected Readings for Individuals & Groups*. San Francisco: HarperSanFrancisco, 1993.

Francis, St. *The Writings of St. Francis of Assisi*. Translated by Paschal Robinson. Sacred Texts. 1905. https://www.sacred-texts.com/chr/wosf/wosf12.htm.

Gaillard, Frye. *A Hard Rain: American in the 1960s, Our Decade of Hope, Possibility, and Innocence Lost*. Montgomery, AL: NewSouth Books, 2018.

Harnish, James. *All I Want for Christmas: An Advent Study for Adults*. Nashville: Abingdon, 2003.

———. *Finding Your Bearings*. Eugene, OR: Cascade, 2021.

———. *When God Comes Down: An Advent Study for Adults*. Nashville: Abingdon, 2012.

Job, Reuben P., and Norman Shawchuck, eds. *A Guide to Prayer for All God's People*. Nashville: Upper Room, 1990.

Jones, E. Stanley. *The Christ of the American Road*. Nashville: Abingdon, 1944.

Bibliography

———. *The Way*. Nashville: Abingdon, 1947.

Kolodiejchuk, Brian, ed. *Mother Teresa: Come Be My Light*. New York: Doubleday, 2007.

Larson, Jonathan. "Seasons of Love [From Rent] Lyrics." Lyrics.com, 2007. https://www.lyrics.com/lyric/12771684/Jonathan+Larson/Seasons+of+Love.

Laymon, Charles M., ed. *The Interpreters One-Volume Commentary on the Bible*. Nashville: Abingdon, 1971.

Lewis, C. S. *The Last Battle*. New York: Collier, 1973.

———. *Mere Christianity*. New York: Touchstone, 1996.

Lincoln, Abraham. "Gettysburg Address." Delivered at Gettysburg, Pennsylvania, November 19, 1863. Library of Congress. https://www.loc.gov/resource/rbpe.24404500/?st=text.

Lischer, Richard. "King's Letter to an Unfaithful Church." *The Christian Century*, April 12, 2023. https://www.christiancentury.org/article/features/white-church-still-owes-letter-birmingham-jail-answer.

Longfellow, Henry Wadsworth. "I Heard the Bells on Christmas Day." Hymnology Archive, December 17, 2019. https://www.hymnologyarchive.com/i-heard-the-bells-on-christmas-day.

Longfellow, Samuel. "Holy Spirit, Truth Divine." Hymnary, n.d. https://hymnary.org/text/holy_spirit_truth_divine_dawn_upon_this.

Maine, Henry James Sumner. *Dissertations on Early Law and Custom*. London: John Murray, 1883. https://oll.libertyfund.org/titles/maine-dissertations-on-early-law-and-custom.

Manskar, Steve. "Glory to God on High, and Peace on Earth Descend." *Discipleship Ministries*, December 24, 2013. https://www.umcdiscipleship.org/blog/glory-to-god-on-high-and-peace-on-earth-descend.

———. "No Holiness but Social Holiness." *Discipleship Ministries*, November 16, 2015. https://www.umcdiscipleship.org/blog/no-holiness-but-social-holiness.

Martin, Phillip. "One of the Exiled Tennessee Legislators Has His Boston Church Standing Behind Him." *GBH News*, April 10, 2023. https://www.wgbh.org/news/national-news/2023/04/10/one-of-the-exiled-tennessee-legislators-has-his-boston-church-standing-behind-him.

McDonnell, Thomas P., ed. *A Thomas Merton Reader*. New York: Doubleday, 1974.

Meacham, Jon. *And There Was Light: Abraham Lincoln and the American Struggle*. New York: Random House, 2022.

Menninger, Karl. *Whatever Became of Sin?* New York: Hawthorne, 1973.

Merton, Thomas. *The Seven Storey Mountain*. New York: Harcourt Brace Jovanovich, 1976.

Moltmann, Jurgen. *In the End—The Beginning*. Minneapolis: Fortress, 2004.

Murray, Hannah. "The Cellist of Sarajevo." *The Active Violinist*, August 31, 2019. https://www.activeviolinist.com/blog/the-cellist-of-sarajevo.

Neal, Jerusha Matsen. *The Overshadowed Preacher: Mary, the Spirit, and the Labor of Proclamation*. Grand Rapids: Eerdmans, 2020.

Bibliography

Overbye, Dennis, and Joey Roulette. "James Webb Space Telescope Launches on Journey to See the Dawn of Starlight." *The New York Times*, December 25, 2021. https://www.nytimes.com/2021/12/25/science/james-webb-telescope-launch.html?campaign_id=2.

Palmer, Parker. *On the Brink of Everything: Grace, Gravity, and Getting Old.* Oakland, CA: Berret-Koehler, 2018.

Peterson, Eugene. *Christ Plays in Ten Thousand Places.* Grand Rapids: Eerdmans, 2005.

———. *Reversed Thunder: The Revelation of John & the Praying Imagination.* New York: HarperCollins, 1988.

Rowe, C. Kavin. *Christianity's Surprise.* Nashville: Abingdon, 2020.

Shakespeare, William. *King Lear.* Edited by Barbara Mowat et al. Folger Shakespeare Library. https://www.folger.edu/explore/shakespeares-works/king-lear/.

———. *Macbeth.* Edited by Barbara Mowat et al. Folger Shakespeare Library. https://www.folger.edu/explore/shakespeares-works/macbeth/.

Skobtsova, Maria. "Quotes Taken from *Mother Maria Skobtsova: Essential Writings.*" Translated by Richard Pevear and Larissa Volokhonsky. https://ssppglenview.org/wp-content/uploads/2018/03/Mother-Maria-quotes.pdf.

Sokol, Donna Claycomb, and L. Roger Owens. *A New Day in the City.* Nashville: Abingdon, 2017.

Steinbeck, John. *The Grapes of Wrath.* New York: Viking, 1939.

Stephens, Bret. "Pearl Harbor and the Capacity for Surprise." *The New York Times*, December 7, 2021. https://www.nytimes.com/2021/12/07/opinion/pearl-harbor-american-adversaries.html.

Stone, Rachel Marie. *Birthing Hope: Giving Fear to Light.* Downers Grove, IL: InterVarsity, 2018.

Sweet, Leonard. "Amen and Amen: So BE It and So DO It." YouTube Video, 34:49, August 8, 2021. https://www.youtube.com/watch?v=AgFPaSmQpAo.

United Methodist Church. *Book of Discipline.* Nashville: United Methodist Publishing, 2016.

United Methodist Communications. "The Wesleyan Means of Grace." United Methodist Church, n.d. https://www.umc.org/en/content/the-wesleyan-means-of-grace.

Van Biema, David. "Mary, So Contrary." *Time*, December 23, 1996. https://content.time.com/time/subscriber/article/0,33009,985739-3,00.html.

Vasile, Paul M. "We Are All Meant to Be Mothers of God." Blog, December 23, 2015. https://www.paulvasile.com/blog/2015/12/23/we-are-all-meant-to-be-mothers-of-god.

Wallace, Hamilton. "Saying No Is Easier than Saying Yes." Small Business Marketing Consultant, n.d. https://www.smallbusinessmarketingconsultant.com/saying-no-is-easier-than-saying-yes/.

Wang, Amy B. "Senate Chaplain Says Lawmakers Must 'Move Beyond Thoughts and Prayer' after Tenn. Shooting." *The Spokesman*, March 28, 2023.

Bibliography

https://www.spokesman.com/stories/2023/mar/28/senate-chaplain-says-lawmakers-must-move-beyond-th/.

Wesley, Charles. "Let Earth and Heaven Combine." Hymns and Carols of Christmas, n.d. https://www.hymnsandcarolsofchristmas.com/Hymns_and_Carols/let_earth_and_heaven_combine.htm.

———. "They Shall Call His Name Immanuel." Hymnary, n.d. https://hymnary.org/text/let_earth_and_heaven_combine_angels_and_.

Wesley, John. "The General Deliverance." Resource UMC, n.d. https://www.resourceumc.org/en/content/sermon-60-the-general-deliverence.

———. *Wesley's Notes on the Bible*. Christian Classics Ethereal Library, n.d. https://www.ccel.org/ccel/wesley/notes.i.iv.iii.html.

Wilde, Oscar. "The Ballad of Reading Gaol." Poets.org, n.d. https://poets.org/poem/ballad-reading-gaol.

Winner, Lauren F. *Wearing God: Clothing, Laughter, Fire and Other Overlooked Ways of Meeting God*. New York: HarperOne, 2015.

Wolterstorff, Nicholas. *Lament for a Son*. Grand Rapids: Eerdmanns, 1987.

Wright, N. T. *Surprised by Hope: Rethinking Heaven, the Resurrection, and the Mission of the Church*. New York: HarperCollins, 2008.

Young, Carlton R., ed. *The United Methodist Hymnal*. Nashville: Abingdon, 1989.

Made in United States
Orlando, FL
18 November 2024